Diaries of a Cancer SURVIVOR
Thais VanGinhoven

moments
with God

TATE PUBLISHING & Enterprises

Published by Tate Publishing & Enterprises, LLC
127 E. Trade Center Terrace | Mustang, Oklahoma 73064 USA
1.888.361.9473 | www.tatepublishing.com

Tate Publishing is committed to excellence in the publishing industry. The company reflects the philosophy established by the founders, based on Psalm 68:11,
"The Lord gave the word and great was the company of those who published it."

Book design copyright © 2010 by Tate Publishing, LLC. All rights reserved.
Cover design by Kristen Verser
Interior design by Stefanie Rane

Published in the United States of America

ISBN: 978-1-61663-538-1
1. Biography & Autobiography, Personal Memoirs
2. Biography & Autobiography, Women
10.09.13

Dedication

For my children, Matthew and Laurelin. They are gifts from God and always fill me with joy and hope.

For my father, Doug Ehman, who said, "When you see white, puffy clouds, you know that good things are ahead."

Acknowledgments

These diaries are my daily log of life. They could never have become this book without many conversations with God. To God, I owe the glory of my life.

With the love and caring nature of family and friends here on this earth, my physical needs were met to survive. My family members have picked me up and carried me through another day when I didn't always feel that I could physically go another step. My children, Matthew and Laurelin, have been and continue to be walking next to me, offering support, love, and joy. They have truly been gifts from God. My mother, Shirley, always has an ear to listen; my father, Doug, taught me how to live and die. My sisters, Erin and Claudia, spent many a late night on the phone with me, and my brothers, Doug and Todd, were the ever-constant men in my life. I couldn't have written this book without all of them and their families, who gave up time and offered prayers daily to assist me.

Thank you to all of the friends who have offered me support and encouragement on a daily basis. My dear friends Jane and Ted's journey has intertwined with mine, Dawn knew that my journey would be with God. With a smile on her face, she offered me my first journal, "To write down the wonderful things that God will do in your life." Dawn and I have had and continue to have conversations for hours, discussing how God works in our daily lives. She is constantly a friend and spiritual mentor. My friend Jeanne took the time from her family and busy daily schedule to take that first trip with me to University of Michigan when others would not go for the evaluation. She continues to stand by my side with unfailing support, as does Shari, who is also a constant friend. Thank you to my friend Jan who is a mentor in life.

A special thank-you to Karen, my sister-in-law, and Proverbs 31 Ministries, who through the *She Speaks* writers and speakers conference gave me the encouragement to pursue what seemed at the time an insurmountable endeavor.

I acknowledge my friend, Jerry Ford, who spent many an hour assisting me in the reading and revision process. Thank you to Michael Overbeek photography studios.

To my dear friend John, a warm heartfelt thank you for gracefully becoming my messenger from God.

This book would not be possible without the countless cards, words of encouragement, and kind ears that have listened throughout these years of treatment, life, and the endeavor of writing a book. To all of you, my family, friends, doctors, nurses, physical therapists, and mentors who have treated me, listened, and offered understanding and encouragement. I am forever grateful.

I continue to acknowledge and pray for healing of others who have gone through similar circumstances—for them and their families. I pray that they may find the strength in God that I have.

To Tate Publishing, A special thank-you for their patience and guidance.

Table of Contents

Introduction

I had a great childhood with two wonderful parents, two sisters, and two brothers. One of my earliest feelings that there must be a God happened when I was young. We, as a family, went sledding at the local snow hill. This always included our family toboggan that was six feet long. This toboggan had been passed down through our family for over one hundred years. On occasion, after sledding the winter would rage around us as we would sit in the snow waiting for hotdogs and marshmallows to grill. My sisters, brothers and myself would watch huge snowflakes fall, trying to catch each one in our mouths. I have warm memories of these times. Often our laughter would bring tears of joy. There had to be a God. Nature was awesome and my family was joyful.

As I grew up, I prayed nightly for all of my family's health and safety. I usually would sneak in a prayer for a horse. I had been told as a small child that if you saw a horse that was snow white, you could make a wish on it and the wish would come true. I did this for years and years; and of course, *every* wish had been for a horse. The years moved on, and my horse never came.

An early moment that turned my life toward God came when I was about fifteen years old. That year, I was able to attend a Christian church camp for youth at Lake Louise. Lake Louise is situated in the ancient forests and clear lakes of northern Michigan, where the air is clear and the water is pristine, eagles soar, and the sunsets are God-inspired. This was going to be a great experience because it was one week away from home, in a beautiful setting of lakes, woods, hills, and no parents. I went to camp looking for boys that summer and found God instead.

God found me in the small, stone chapel on the hill in the woods. The morning mist was engulfing the tiny structure, and one ray of morning sunshine fell onto the floor. I sat by myself and declared to God that I wanted to follow in His footsteps. At this same moment, my roommate began to play the wind whistle in our cabin at the foot of the hill. She played softly and beautifully as I gave my heart to Jesus.

In my teenage years, I began to journal, a practice I continue with today. This helped me grow spiritually by writing down God's experiences in my life. I attended church, Bible studies and prayed daily for family and others in difficult situations. Of course, as I grew, I began to pray that someday, God would send to me a handsome and loving man to spend my entire life with. Then, one day, I looked up and smiled. *He* was standing there. I experienced years of happiness, joy, tears and sorrow with my husband; and then through so many prayers, two wonderful gifts and miracles from God arrived into our lives—our children, Matthew and Laurelin.

I still had a feeling that my spiritual life fell short, although I was very blessed by God. Was I worthy of His blessings? Had I, as a follower of Christ, been doing enough? My days with God waxed and waned like the moon. I was never quite experiencing the intensity with God and the closeness I had felt in that chapel on the hill in the woods, surrounded by God and the mist. What was I missing?

In the years that followed, there were job changes for moving up the ladder, homes that didn't sell, new friends to meet, and new schools to attend. There were changes one after another. I think they call it *life*, those things that you hadn't thought about encountering. Going through difficult times would make our family become even closer, right? I was soon to find that Tad had other thoughts.

We purchased and built our first home on four acres very close to Lake Michigan after renting for thirteen years of marriage. We had built this home together with the dream of raising our family there. The undertaking took time from our jobs and family but we saved money doing much of it on our own. It was a work of love, blood, sweat and tears.

We lived there less than two years. Tad was offered the job of a lifetime, the dream job. The only problem was that it required moving and giving up our dream of raising our family in the home we had built. We staked the real estate sign in the yard, packed a few items and together we set off on the new adventure.

One day, years later God showed me in Technicolor what was missing in my life. I began a journey that included cancer, laughter, tears, death, life, the beginning of new relationships and the end of others.

These are my diaries of that journey. At times I write with complete cohesiveness other entries are disjointed due to chemo, steroids, exhaustion, fear of the unknown and stress. My thoughts can be incomplete and fleeting hopping in and out of my consciousness like Peter Rabbit let loose in Mr. McGregor's garden.

Months before being diagnosed with cancer I had broken my foot. I continued for weeks during the healing process to work as a dental hygienist maneuvering on crutches and wearing a cast. The day my cast was taken off I was exhausted. It was that same day I received the message that my healthy father had suffered a massive stroke. Within hours of his stroke I stood with my mother at the foot of my father's hospital bed and heard the words, "Your husband may not talk, walk or live beyond this week." This was my mother's mate of 50 years and my father who was lying paralyzed in the hospital bed. I reassured my mother that I would make the hour and a half drive to be there to support both of them. My parents had always supported and loved me now it was time to help them.

In the next four months that followed I began to see cracks in my marriage of over 25 years. We had seemed to weather life well together when the sailing was smooth but rough sailing was something Tad had never mastered. The storms of life were beginning to form a fissure between my husband and myself. I maintained my job working my regular hours. I continued to care for my family and home while supporting my mother and father in the nightmare that was unfolding.

I began this journey with God the day I held out my hand and he reached to encompass mine. He has been holding my hand each and every step, each and every day.

It wasn't a journey that I would have chosen for myself, but I now pray daily that my journey with God never ends. It has been a challenge, but I have surrendered. These diaries chronicle that journey. I call them my *Moments with God* and I look forward to sharing them with you.

My Journey Begins

Thursday, November 21, 2002
cold, drizzle of rain, very gray day, thirty five degrees

Today on my agenda, I will have my routine mammogram at 8:00 a.m. I will be off for other errands after my appointment. Oh yes. I have a day off of work so that I can catch up on all of the things that aren't getting done.

Tomorrow, my husband, Tad, and I will join our daughter, Laurelin, and her boyfriend, Travis, to tour the Hope College campus in Holland, Michigan. Our son, Matthew, is already gone now to college; and Laurelin, our youngest, will be gone next year. Tad and I will be starting together a new part of our lives. We have saved and worked many jobs so we can retire early. This should be a fun adventure to have together after working for so many years.

It will then be time to take trips together. Tad had promised, for twelve years, that we would soon take another trip to Europe, tropical islands, skiing, and Bermuda. He had been to Bermuda on business, and I hadn't. Bermuda was where we had planned to take our honeymoon. My family had come from there. Tad had researched it; and he had thought it to be too expensive, so other, and less expensive, plans were made for the honeymoon. Tad had recently been given the chance for free to travel to Bermuda for a board meeting of five days' duration. Much of the trip had been set aside for free time. The trip was free, and others were taking their spouses and paying the difference for the airfare. Tad thought it best that I stayed home from that trip.

Now all of that would be behind us, and we could just pick up and go and play golf as we wanted to—do all of those things that we had worked and saved our entire lives for. Tad could work a few days a week if he wanted, and it would be less stressful. Retirement; we are almost to that future day. We have always been working for the future and now the future is almost here.

I've never really been on the beautiful and historic campus of Hope College. They have artistic performances, such as a theater and chorale; but Tad is not interested in those things on the campus. I have not had the opportunity like Tad has to attend sporting events or meetings that are held on the campus. The tour will be a good thing. I am really tired, and I don't want to go to have my mammogram today. In my head, I hear the voices of friends that have had cancer in the past that are ringing in my ears. The voices call out, "You have to go. That is the only way that I found my cancer."

Today, I'll go for the voices of my friends—even though I am exhausted.

11:00 a.m.

The nursing staff at the office of the doctors who performed the mammogram this morning called my home two hours after the procedure and asked if I would please return the call as soon as possible. I most likely left something there. I returned the phone call. No, I did not leave something there.

I need a new mammogram and other films and an ultrasound. Choices for dates are tomorrow or three and a half weeks. Well, tomorrow is Laurelin's college day; but three and a half weeks is a long time to wait. I will have to explain to Laurelin that I may be a little late. Travis, Laurelin's boyfriend, and Tad, who is my husband and her father, should be there.

Friday, November 22, 2002
dark and rainy

My appointment was scheduled early in the morning, and how I would have loved to sleep in today. The weather is dark and rainy, a typical day in November in Michigan: lousy.

Today, as I had my second mammogram and a physical exam, I noticed that everyone was quiet. No one was laughing and talking about children and parents coming home for the Thanksgiving holiday like they had been yesterday.

All of the tests had been finished, and the nurse said that she would show the completed tests to the doctor. I just needed to wait, naked, in my hospital gown that didn't close in the back with my butt freezing. I waited, for what seemed an eternity.

Then I met a tall, striking man named Dr. Tallerman. He walked into my room with a long face, no happiness in his eyes, and said, "All of the tests are very suspicious. You need a biopsy of your right breast, a needle core biopsy." He went on to explain the procedure. "It is a biopsy taken with a hollow needle about the thickness of the lead inside of a pencil. This needle is injected into your breast when you are numb, at the correct area that is found with ultrasound. After being injected, the needle is removed quickly, retrieving a tissue biopsy within the hollow needle. Six of these are needed to be tested by the lab. And if it shows cancer, it is typed by the lab as to what kind of cancer the biopsy shows."

"Tuesday will be available with no waiting," he said. "Do you have any questions?"

"No," was all I could say.

"You can dress now, and we will schedule the appointment." The door closed behind him with a thud.

I sat by myself, staring at the wall, thinking, *just get dressed. Get dressed.* The word *cancer* crept into the cracks that were forming inside my mind. *Cancer? Get dressed.*

With my next appointment scheduled, I was then off to Hope College for the great college walk and tour. I met up with Laurelin, Travis, and Tad in the beautiful stone chapel on campus. It was made strong to endure the ages. This was a fortress. It was a place of God where I could hide, a place of strength where I could comprehend the magnitude of what had just happened and what might be revealed with the next set of information that the doctor would collect. The windows were made of exquisitely placed, vibrant-colored glass that showed stories from the Bible. The new students and their parents filled the chapel, and I slid in next to Laurelin, onto the beautiful, deeply worn, wooden pew. I saw that she was happy and holding onto Travis's hand.

Tad knew that I had been to have a biopsy and would possibly be late. Why did he look so angry? Was it because I was late? We sang the song "Promise of His Love," and I realized that I most likely had cancer; it hit me, sitting in the house of the Lord, that God would protect me. I shed tears in God's beautiful chapel.

Laurelin had no idea of what I was doing at my doctor's appointment that had made me late. She thought that I was overwhelmed by the church's beauty and the hopeful song that was chosen. *Yes, it is that, and I may have cancer.* I gave her a smile, said a prayer, and went on to the rest of the college tour.

Saturday, November 23, 2002

I went to see my friend Jan in the hospital. She had breast cancer not long ago; and before she could really heal from that, she has had a terrible bout with colon problems. She is not doing well. She may need another major surgery. She looks so frail and thin. She is a fighter with a great support group of husband, children, friends, and parents. I couldn't tell her about me. She is too sick. I went home and tried to collect all the data from friends that have had cancer before me. I told Tad what I had discovered at the doctors: I may have cancer and I need a biopsy soon. No hugs, no questions. He just stared at me.

Tad has never been one to be available for someone if they needed comfort, unless it comforted him. I have always wondered if it is the stoic Dutch heritage or if he just has no empathy for those he loves. Or is there something there even deeper and darker that I don't know about? He didn't offer to, and doesn't want to, come with me to the biopsy appointment, so I will go alone. I called my friend Sue, who has had cancer, to see if she could answer any of the questions I have or calm this storm building inside of me. She wasn't home. I left a message, trying to sound as calm and cool as you can when you see a tidal wave approaching you.

Sunday, November 24, 2002
rain, cold, dark, thirty four degrees

Sue called me back. She asked for all the information that I had. We talked on the phone for an hour as she explained how her biopsy had been taken and went on to explain that there was more than one way to do a biopsy. She insisted on coming to my appointment. She would not let me go alone.

Monday, November 25, 2002 (Thanksgiving Week)

At work, I had to try to rearrange my schedule to allow for the biopsy to be done tomorrow. I had explained to the doctors I worked for that I needed a cancer biopsy done as soon as possible. They understood the need to rearrange my schedule. Now they had to reschedule patients with phone calls and more phone calls and I may possibly have cancer.

Today, I returned to a friend the Lance Armstrong book about his trials with cancer. Also I returned to another friend the book *Tuesdays with Morrie*. This was a book about a student who, when he finds out that his past instructor is dying of cancer, visits once a week until his death. Both books had been given to me randomly to read within the last months by separate friends. Could God have been the guiding arm in delivering these books to me to prepare me for my future? At this time, the only people who know that I am having a cancer biopsy are Tad, Sue, and the doctors that I work for. I'm exhausted. I need to see Mom and Dad, and I need a biopsy for cancer. What a day.

Then my mind turned to what Mom, Dad and I had been going through during the last four months. Tonight I am exhausted just thinking about what has been happening. I have been driving over one hour each way to and from St.

Joseph, trying to help Mom and Dad. I am just now able to write in my journal about what has been happening in my life.

My father, Doug Ehman, had a devastating stroke on August 1, 2002, about four months ago. I found out about his stroke the day I had a cast removed from my broken foot. Now, since August I work four days a week and I travel daily after working to try to help Dad and Mom.

Dad's stroke left him completely paralyzed for a number of days. I found it so hard to see my father not able to move and barely able to say a word. He has always been a man of few words, but the words he said were always important and well thought out. I could see the terror in his eyes as he realized that he was not in control of his own body. I loved to watch how his eyes would soften when I gave him a kiss and held his hand. This was my father, who had carried me on his shoulders and pulled me on the sled and wagon. *My Dad*, the one and only. He would let me sleep those few precious extra moments in the morning before school and ultimately I would miss the bus. He would always be there to take me to school.

In the hospital I had run my fingers through my father's hair remembering his bear hugs. His arms were large and his hugs could completely engulf me and my two sisters when we were small. He would squeeze gently until we laughed; yet, he was as gentle and as caring as if he had picked up a baby bird to replace it to its mothers nest. He would let us three girls mess with his hair, what he had of it, combing, curling and styling it for hours on end. In those first few days in the hospital he was remote, distant, and tied up to monitors. The sterile smell of a hospital made it hard to remember his hugs and tickles.

Mom was a wreck. She wanted to control everything. Before she retired, she was the house supervisor of nursing at that hospital. It was hard for her to realize that she no longer was in that position. I had to remember that she was Dad's only advocate and wife of more than fifty one years. I prayed that I will have an advocate if I lie in the hospital, paralyzed like he was. Dad didn't want her to leave his side, but she was having some serious acute health problems that needed to be addressed at that time. In the hospital, Mom went to the emergency room; she needed bed rest, medicine and treatment. When Mom left, Dad was overwhelmed with stress and despair. She had always been his sounding board, his pillar of strength, his confidant.

I was able to stay with Dad in the hospital day and night for a few days while Mom healed. I held Dad's hand, and he breathed a little easier. I needed to be there to hold Mom's hand also. Who was holding my hand in all of this uncertainty, despair, and complete utter chaos?

On many days, the nurses would move a wooden bench closer to Daddy so that I could rest while holding his hand. Once in awhile, we would have a few silent moments without interruption. I could at that time lay down, take Daddy's hand in mine, quietly rest and pray for Dad, Mom and myself.

I could hear our rhythmic breathing: in, out, in, out; one, two, one, two. I noticed that as my breath moved in and out of my lungs, my foot would throb more painfully with each passing minute. At that point I had only been off crutches two weeks, and the healing fracture of four bones had been screaming at me. I rested in and out of consciousness with my father's hand in mine. Again, I wondered who would hold my hand and comfort me. Then I realized that it was my Father in heaven who had been holding my hand. On that night this brought me total, relaxing, deep rest. God was by my side holding my hand. This was how I had been able to deal with all of the confusion and absolute utter chaos. A complete peace came over me of being one with God and knowing that he was there by my side and my father's side each and every moment.

Those next days brought only more tests and no answers about Dad's future. He was having great difficulty breathing and swallowing. Every passing day brought with it more chaos, more tests, less information, despair, and complete exhaustion for all three of us.

Mom was still being treated for her illness. She was unable to be by Dad's side every day, yet she offered support each second that she could. On one particular day, my heart was less burdened. The night before, I had fallen into a deep sleep and dreamed that I was cradled in God's arms. This induced for me a profound, restful sleep. Somehow, I felt that I had to get Dad to feel what I did.

Now it has been four months of keeping up my home, trying to help Mom and Dad after working all day and now it appears as though I may have cancer. God, you know all things, could you give a hint of what the days will be like that follow this one?

Tonight, I opened my Bible and read these verses.

> Those who know your name will trust in you, for you Lord have never forsaken those who seek you.
>
> Psalm 9: 10–11

> For you created my inmost being; you knit me together in my mother's womb. I praise you because I am fearfully and wonderfully made; your works are wonderful, I know that full well. My frame was not hidden from you when I was made in the secret place. When I was woven together in the depths of the earth, your eyes saw my unformed body. All the days ordained for me were written in your book before one of them came to be. How precious to me are your thoughts, O God! How vast is the sum of them! Were I to count them, they would out number the grains of sand. When I awake, I am still with you.
>
> Psalm 139: 13–18

Biopsy

Tuesday, November 26, 2002
raw, cold, rainy, wet, twenty eight degrees

Sue and I met at my doctor's office, and she brought me some brightly colored flowers. I'm actually glad that someone was with me for this six-core biopsy. Sue had explained what might happen for the biopsy procedure. This is the reality.

There is a steel table with two holes (one for each breast to hang through), a computer, an ultrasound machine, a doctor, and two assistants. Dr. Tallerman nicely reintroduced himself and asked if I had any questions. In my head, I was thinking, *is this a dream?* Instead I said, "No questions." Dr. Tallerman patiently waited while the assistants helped me slip off my gown to waist level and positioned me on the steel table that was as cold as death. They helped me lay down on the steel table face-first. It felt like I was hugging a cold steel refrigerator. The goose bumps covered my entire body. I was now lying on the steel table with my breasts through the two holes. My head was turned, and my eyes were intently watching my doctor. I could hear the computer humming in the background.

Dr. Tallerman sat on his stool and smiled. He slid on his stool over next to me. He said, "I will raise the hydraulic table and begin the procedure." The table was raised and Dr. Tallerman, equipment in hand, sitting on his stool, slid underneath my body.

He was so tall that he had to duck, bend, and contort his upper body under the table so as not to hit his head. With instruments in hand and his body twisting and turning to find the correct position, I felt he was definitely multi-tasking. I said to him, "Do you feel a little like an auto mechanic?" He burst out laughing. The tension in the room was broken.

I was given injections of anesthetic to get numb before they removed the six hollow core biopsies from my breast.

"Okay. Ready?"

"Yikes!" I could feel that one to my toes. I was *not* numb. The doctor was very apologetic and gave me more anesthetic. The next five biopsies were without pain. Doctor Tallerman wheeled out from underneath me and placed the biopsies on a clean gauze square.

As the steel table on which I laid was lowered, I saw the biopsies that were sitting on the gauze. I am a medical person; and as I stood up, it dawned on me that I didn't want it to be contaminated. Maybe it should be enclosed in glass or something sterile. Then I realized it wouldn't matter if it were contaminated; it would still come up cancerous or non-cancerous.

I asked Dr. Tallerman as I stood and looked at the color and texture of the sample, "What does a biopsy of cancer look like?" A total hush came over the room, and the doctor gave a description of a typical cancer biopsy. The description he gave seemed to match, detail for detail, *my* biopsy that lay in front of me on that gauze square.

He never said, "You have cancer." But I believed that this was the beginning of a very long journey. I was glad that Sue came with me. She helped me steady myself and walk out of the office. We talked in the parking lot for a long time. Then, when I was mentally clear enough to drive, we went to lunch. God had given me this dear friend who had been down this road to help me on this journey I might be starting today.

The samples were rushed today after the biopsy was taken by 4 p.m. to the lab. Dr. Tallerman said, "The results should be back by tomorrow, Wednesday." I thought to myself that since it was a holiday weekend the lab may not have it completed. The lab techs would all be trying to finish early to have precious time to visit families' homes for the holiday. I thought to myself, *Thais, be patient.*

It was very difficult, but today I told my daughter, Laurelin, in a moment of quiet time, that I had just had a biopsy for breast cancer. I have had a couple of days for the possibility of cancer to settle in my mind and heart. It seems to be helping me. I am glad that I have had time to think, time to take it all in. I hope that it works this way for the children. I saw complete shock, love, and concern from Laurelin. We hugged each other tightly as the tears flowed between us like a river. My breast ached, and I prayed that my daughter would never have to feel the pain that was growing in my mind and the physical hurt that I was feeling in my breast. Maybe if she also can digest it a little at a time before we find out for sure it will be easier and we'll all be more prepared.

Matt is still at college. I couldn't call him and blurt it over the phone. I'll have to talk to him tomorrow when he gets home. I want this to be as painless as possible for both of them.

Wednesday, November 27, 2002
cold, bright day with ominous clouds.

This is the day before Thanksgiving. This morning, and every morning begins with a walk out to the barn to see my horses, to greet them with kind words and to hear their soft morning knickers and whinnies. I would stroke their necks as they rubbed into my body with 1200 pounds of love and affection. I drove to work thinking about my life. Thinking about the thousands of drives I have made to work from our beautiful home in the country, thinking of how this drive had always brought to me a comfort as I drove through farmland, past the animals grazing and the crops growing from seeds in the fields that would be harvested. For years, I had appreciated the morning mist on the fields and the evening shadows along acres of wheat and corn. I usually liked the light traffic for the first twenty minutes of the drive, and every day God showed me a new canvas that he was painting for my day. Then, after twenty minutes, I would be in the traffic of the city and ready to be in a day full of people. Some days, after work, I would have my bike with me and ride for twenty miles along the Lake Michigan shoreline, enjoying the perfect summer days and the gentle breezes that the lake brings. I lived in an ideal place.

This morning as I was driving into work I happened to look toward the east. The sunrise was one of the most beautiful I have ever seen in my life. The eastern sky was on fire with brilliant reds, flaming vermillion, and shooting pinks. There was constant movement in the most vibrant purples and violets bursting with radiance. It was gorgeous.

I thought to myself, *God has done this for me! This is a gift for* me *today, in these few fleeting seconds that I happened to look.* The tears welled in my eyes. I've often heard that God will come from the East to take us home; and it very shortly crossed my mind that this might be it, the going home. So I stopped the car on the side of the road and thought for a moment. I wondered about what God would see in the West when he came to take us home. I got out of the car so that I could look in all directions, and I turned to face west. I gazed upon the most beautiful continuation of God's morning artwork.

The sky in the west was the deepest and most brilliant purples, pinks, reds, indigos, and blues, all undulating and moving with God's breath. A 360-degree turn showed me the magnitude of God's glory at that second in time in that earthly place. These verses came to mind.

> For the Lord God is a sun and shield; the Lord bestows favor and honor; no good thing does he withhold from those whose walk is blameless.
>
> Psalm 84: 11

> The Lord is compassionate and gracious; slow to anger, abounding in love. He will not always accuse, nor will he harbor his anger forever; he does not treat us as our sins deserve or repay us according to our iniquities. For as high as the heavens are above the earth, so great is his love for those who fear him; as far as the east is from the west, so far has he removed our transgressions from us. As a father has compassion on his children, so the Lord has compassion on those who fear him; for he knows how we are formed, he remembers that we are dust. As for man his days are like grass, he flourishes like a flower of the field: the wind blows over it and it is gone, and its place remembers it no more. But from everlasting to everlasting the Lords love is with those who fear him and his righteousness with their children's children with those who keep his covenant and remember to obey his precepts. The Lord has established his throne in heaven, and his kingdom rules over all.
>
> Psalm 103:8–19

I realized that I would be loved and cared for whether I had cancer or not. This was God's reminder that he will always be with me each step of the way through life and death. A great calm came over me. I looked to the east; the colors were gone, but my heart was full of God's grace.

I had been instructed to call the lab during the day about the biopsy. I called repeatedly. No information yet.

When driving home after working, the deep November clouds opened, and rays of the most dramatic sunshine poured down as if to light my way. The sun rays were very intensely bright, and it looked as if they could be slides for angels to come to Earth. In my heart, I have a deep feeling that I have cancer. An intense, peaceful calm came over my soul. I knew not to worry and to not be upset, for God already knows the outcome. Worrying will not help the situation. I must be strong and rely on God. At that moment I thought of one of my favorite verses.

> Therefore I tell you, do not worry about your life, what you will eat or drink; or about your body, what you will wear. Is not life more important than food, and the body more important than clothes? Look at the birds of the air; they do not sow or reap or store away in barns, and yet your heavenly father feeds them. Are you not much more valuable than they?
>
> Who of you by worrying can add a single hour to his life?
>
> Matthew 6: 27

The biopsy was not ready today. Now I won't find out until November 29. That will be my twenty-seventh wedding anniversary. What a present. We will also all have to get through the Thanksgiving holiday without knowing if I have cancer.

Matt came home today from college and heard me on the phone talking with my friend. When I hung up, Matt was gone, and I asked Tad, "Where did Matt go?"

Tad said, "He's upstairs, talking to Laurelin in her room."

When Matt came down I asked him, "Do you have any questions?"

His reply was, "About what?"

I told him what was going on, that I had a biopsy and the possibility of cancer. He had no idea. I saw the same total shock, love, and concern that I had seen on Laurelin's face. He hugged me, and we sat down with tears in our eyes. Matt asked all of the questions on his heart. His first question was, "Mom will you be okay and what can I do to help?" We talked for hours into the night.

Thanksgiving, November 28, 2002
sunny, clear, fifty degrees

I can't help but think about it, but I feel so at peace. Last night, Matthew, Laurelin, and I laughed and made pies together for today's meal. We set the table together for a feast of Thanksgiving. Today, things fell into place well. Mom and Dad wanted to stay home in Stevensville instead of coming to our home as they have done in the past. Dad is still so bad from his stroke, and Mom is preparing to take them both to Florida for the winter. It is hard for them to pick up and move. They are exhausted.

We had a wonderful dinner with great food, family, and friends. I have had such happiness. Matt's friend, Alli, and Travis came over and played euchre with our entire family. We even had a euchre tournament. Who cares who won? Everyone had a great time. What a complete day of thanksgiving to God's glory. This won't be my last Thanksgiving with my family. I will need to be a very tough fighter and come out of this much stronger and not alone.

Waiting and Still Waiting

Friday, November 29, 2002
rather cold, damp, winter day with little snow and no sunshine

It is very quiet in the house. I called Holland Mammography at 9:00 a.m., and the biopsy is not completed yet. An office worker suggested that I call back in one hour. I did. The nurse said, "Dr. Tallerman would like to talk to you personally this afternoon." This did not sound good at all. I needed a diversion. I went to the barn to see my two horses and then out shopping for Christmas.

Will this be my last Christmas? Dr. Tallerman, my doctor, called me at the house in the afternoon while Tad, Matt, Laurelin, and I were decorating the tree. I took the call by myself in the bedroom. His words were, "Thais, I wish that I had better news, but you have cancer." I can't say that I am surprised. I have had some time to think about that word. *Cancer.*

He suggested that I find a surgeon soon and could help recommend someone if I had no idea who to call. It seems to be a rather aggressive type of cancer. The rest of the biopsy needs to be sent to Mayo Clinic, where they can finish typing it. I needed to tell Tad, Matt, Laurelin, Mom, Dad, and my brothers and sisters. I also should call Sue. She would want to know the diagnosis. After all, she was the one who went with me to the biopsy.

Dr. Tallerman and I talked for awhile. He was considerate, and I was calm and in shock. When I returned to the Christmas tree, Tad had left. I told Matt and Laurelin. "Yes, I do have cancer and will need surgery and possibly chemo and radiation soon." Their eyes filled full of tears, and their arms were warm and inviting with big hugs. Great support and love came from them both. They were both on the phone right away. Everyone needs to tell someone.

I found Tad in the garage. I told Tad. He looked at me, hugged me lightly, and said, "I'm sorry." Then, in the same breath, he said, "You'll have to sell the horses now. You won't be able to pay for them." Amazing. He didn't say anything about dropping the country club. I just stared into space as he walked away. *Happy Anniversary, Thais.* Later that day I went to the barn to see my horses. I caressed Khanada's and Laddie's thick necks and their warm, soft fur, and I sobbed, holding on to them tightly and feeling the warmth of their bodies. They stood, and each wrapped their large, long necks around my body as if to hug and comfort me. They both held me close.

Saturday, November 30, 2002
cool, cloudy, a little sun, forty three degrees

I went for a horseback ride on my long lean thoroughbred retired race horses. Laddie was a dream; and Khanada was a good, strong girl. It amazes me the power and gentleness that is in one of God's huge animals. Their bodies are warm and soft, and they move with every flicker of each of my muscles. Their response is so relaxed, and they soften their muscles with mine. I love my time with them because when I ride, I don't think of anything but the horses and myself as one. There are no thoughts of the surgeon, no thoughts of cancer, no thoughts of the future, and no thoughts of dying or staying alive; there are just the thoughts about how it is great to be alive today on God's earth with these two wonderful animals.

Sunday, December 1, 2002
another gloomy day

I went to see my friend Jan again in the hospital. She has already battled breast cancer and now serious, life-threatening health issues about her intestines and colon. She needs to feel better, and soon. I pray each day for her.

Wednesday, December 4, 2002
sun poking its head out, thirty four degrees

Another friend, Deb that had been diagnosed with cancer about one month ago had told me about the University of Michigan. She said that they have a breast clinic where about eight doctors digest all of your information and make a comprehensive decision about your total treatment.

Tad and I went to see two surgeons locally for evaluation of the surgery. They have given me the choice of a lumpectomy or a mastectomy. I do know that if a lumpectomy is performed and all of the cancer is removed on the first surgery, it will be less invasive but may require more treatment with chemo and radiation. If a mastectomy is performed, the entire breast is removed and all of the cancer is removed with the surgery. There would then be reconstruction, but possibly less radiation and chemo are needed.

The surgeons cannot make decisions about treatment after removal of the cancer. It is not their expertise. They have no idea what other treatment that I may need. I would have to talk with the doctor of radiation and chemotherapy.

What is a person to do? I want to know the complete picture. I think I will check into *all* the possibilities for thorough and complete treatment. The University of Michigan is on my list, although they only do these clinics on Mondays. Next Friday I have surgery set up in Grand Rapids with a man that is a good surgeon but has no idea what I need after I choose which surgery I want. That's easy. I don't want any surgery. I'm not feeling very confident with having an incomplete picture of treatment in front of me before I start the surgery in Grand Rapids.

Today, I was at work and equipped with the phone number for the University of Michigan's breast clinic. At 8:00 a.m. exactly, I called them and spoke with Lilly, a scheduler for the University of Michigan. I explained my need to get into the clinic as soon as possible. It was explained to me that there were no openings for six weeks.

Six weeks! Don't they know that this is life or death? It happens to be *my* life or death! What were they thinking? She suggested that I call back and she would let me have the first cancellation. Okay. I can do that. I work in a medical office, and I know that people cancel medical appointments. So today, all day long, I called my newest and best friend at the University of Michigan between every one of my patients—about every half hour. We really got to know each other.

At 3:00 p.m., I spoke with Lilly, and she said, "Someone just cancelled for this Monday." The appointment was mine! The only catch is that all slides, x-rays, biopsy reports, CT scans and mammograms from the last three years need to be there at 7:00 a.m. on this Friday. It was Wednesday at 3:00 p.m., and I was at work. I didn't have in my possession most of those things. I took the appointment with great joy and concern. How would I pull this off?

I called the hospital lab; and the secretary was out, so the lab technician answered. I explained my situation and that I needed all of my information and slides sent to the University of Michigan by 7:00 a.m. on Friday.

She said, "It is impossible. We are *not* finished running all the tests on the slides." I told her that around Thanksgiving I had waited two extra days for the results of my biopsy to come back from their office. Now I needed them to come through for me.

She said, "We will try to get them completed for you."

At 4:53 p.m., I received a call from a worker at the lab that all of the slides would be completed and could be picked up by 6:00 p.m. There was a FedEx drop-off in the town that I lived in, and the last drop-off time was 6:30 p.m. I was overjoyed. Thank you, God. Thank you for this wonderful work in my life. Time was moving faster as I was running through the halls of the hospital to pick up the data and get to FedEx before closing.

When I arrived at the FedEx building to send the information to the University of Michigan, the FedEx woman was locking the door. I told her through the glass doors what I needed.

She opened the door with tears in her eyes and said, "Come in." She told me, "I was on the way to see my brother, who is dying of cancer, so maybe by this one act; I can bring life to someone." She truly is accounting for her fellow mankind.

And for your lifeblood I will surely demand an accounting. I will demand an accounting from every animal. And from each man, too, I will demand an accounting for the life of his fellow man.

Genesis 9: 5

We shared a bear hug that came from the depths or our hearts, and she returned behind the counter to stamp and send my precious information. The package was sent and will be received by the 7:00 a.m. Friday deadline at University of Michigan. My appointment is scheduled for Monday.

Last night, I spoke with Tad to ask him if he would please go with me to University of Michigan if I was able to get an appointment for an evaluation with their board of doctors. He won't go with me. He is afraid that the insurance won't pay for another evaluation. I explained to Tad that I had already called the insurance company and they will pay for another opinion. Tad says that he has appointments at work. It is a three hour trip one-way and a few hours for the evaluation, another full day. He is busy. I'm on my own. As I drove home from the FedEx building, I saw a red truck that rode next to me. In the back window, I read these words: Be still before the Lord and wait patiently for him. (Psalm 37: 7)

What a grand Lord he is. This truck drove directly in front of me for at least ten minutes. God had sent this reminder for me. I read and read again the Psalm verse. I cried buckets of tears and laughed at the same time. I think God took over the driving. It is a reminder from my God in heaven that He is always there for me.

The University of Michigan

Monday, December 9, 2002
cold, mist rising in the fields, twenty eight degrees

I woke up at 4:30 a.m. My dear friend Jeanne, who has been my friend through thick and thin, said that she would go with me to the University of Michigan for the evaluation. Tad won't go, and she feels that two sets of ears and eyes would be better than one; she doesn't want me to go by myself. So Jeanne is here by 6:00 a.m., and we are off for the adventure by 6:15 a.m. The university is rated very high in the United States for the treatment of breast cancer and has a low death rate, but I am only going for a complete opinion about all treatment needed, not to have the actual treatment completed at U of M.

The roads became more slippery as we drove to Ann Arbor, where the University of Michigan is located. There was a fog across the road, but it was cold enough that ice crystals were forming in the road. The road glistened with a thin layer of deadly ice. Jeanne held the steering wheel firmly as my breath grew shallower from anticipation of a slide into the ditch. I began to wonder if this was a good idea. Jeanne was confident at the wheel. The fog broke. The sunrise as we drove into it was beautifully painted on the canvas before our eyes, and it quickly melted all of our fears of traveling on a sheet of ice for three hours.

Once we were in the facility, it was wait and test and test and wait. Many of the people looked so sad and confused. Jeanne and I were talking and giggling, sharing some of our life stories with each other. Another person who was waiting asked if one of us had cancer; and I replied, "I do."

She said, "How can you be so joyful when you know that you may die?"

I thought for a moment, not knowing if this person was a patient or the supporting person of a patient. I was looking for the perfect words to soothe her soul. I said, "That is correct. Someday, I will die. We all will. But today, I have an awesome friend by my side and God holding my hand, and I am at one of the best medical facilities in the country to treat my cancer. Why would I not be joyous?" She stared at the two of us and smiled.

The hospital was collecting information on me for hours, and Jeanne was so patient. We happened to get the head surgeon of all surgical oncology at University of Michigan. *Thank you, God.* I feel even more confident. By 3:30 p.m., we are approached by a research doctor and asked if I would like to be in a clinical study. My first reaction was *no.* I want to find out what conventional treatment is recommended to save my life. Clinical studies, in my mind, are "what if" scenarios. I want concrete treatment that will save me; no "what ifs." But Jeanne and I are both medical people, and we want to hear about it. Good thing we brought the small recorder.

This is called a cryotherapy surgery clinical trial. Cryotherapy is performed by freezing the cancer and, in this case, with an argon gas probe that is inserted into the center of the cancer mass using ultrasound. I seem to meet the standards that the research doctors have set. Scientists and doctors are wondering if by performing cryo three weeks before routine surgery if possibly more margins will be clear and cancer free. The question remains will it stimulate your auto immune system to kick in and begin to make antibodies against the cancer? If so, this would be a great thing. Not to mention that this doctor is absolutely young and good looking. May we call him Dr. Handsome? He has an awesome personality and, might I add, is single. Are there no aged doctors any more, or am I just getting old? Now, with more information, I am considering entering the study. I have many friends that are women, mothers, and sisters; and, of course, there is always my daughter to think about. What if by doing this I could save one of them from this cancer or make their treatment easier?

The study involves an additional appointment and surgery. I would return home and do nothing for three weeks except *wait*. It could be painful. At the three-week point, the patient would do conventional treatment and numerous blood draws.

There are some drawbacks, but I will pray about it. My entire treatment was explained to me by seven doctors. It is an aggressive cancer. Mastectomy? Lumpectomy? The doctors felt that the difference in recurrence was so small that a lumpectomy would be their choice along with a sentinel node biopsy to see if the cancer is in the lymph nodes. Unfortunately, this needs one week for biopsy results. After the clinical study and waiting three weeks, the treatment would include two to three surgeries; about two months of daily radiation; and, of course, I needed chemo for about six months because it was so aggressive. As a kicker, something is unusual with my receptors. This may mean that there is a hidden factor that may not be good. These tests have been sent to the Mayo Clinic, where they can be typed. Then, additional treatment can be planned if needed.

I have unusual receptors? Somehow, I am always in the wrong line. By 6:30 p.m., I was definitely on overload. There are all of these decisions for me to make. God must think I am stronger than I sometimes think that I am. Jeanne and I need a glass of wine and a great dinner. Dr. Handsome makes a restaurant suggestion for Jeanne and me, and ten minutes later, the two of us were there.

This is truly what the doctor ordered: awesome Italian food and fantastic wine, candlelight and soft music, and a mind over-filled with complete information. What a great, long, wonderful day to be alive in God's world with Jeanne by my side.

The three-hour trip home was contemplative and intro-spective. Jeanne and I were both drained, but what a great friend to be drained with. Tonight, I am exhausted. I will sleep deep, pray big, and contemplate it all in the morning. I have cancer in me, but I have hope in fantastic doctors, with options and friends and family that care. Now, rest.

Tuesday, December 10, 2002
amazing sunshine

I called, my new friend, Lilly at the University of Michigan and told her that I want to be a part of the clinical trial. I hadn't realized that there were a certain number of patients that could be accepted for treatment and some patients had to accept no treatment so that the study could have a non-cryo group to be compared to. Well, this was a no-brainer. I want to have the treatment. I slid in just under the wire to be in the clinical trial.

When I arrived home from work, Laurelin was very sick with strep throat; so off we went to the emergency room. It was a long wait. Laurelin rested her head on my shoulder and I smoothed her hair. Laurelin's hair is so beautiful, auburn and shiny like mine; and soon, I won't have any. None. Nothing. I will have no hair to worry about fixing or washing or curling. Well, at least it should cut down on shampoo costs and time getting ready.

As I opened my Bible for comfort at bedtime, I opened to Samuel 2:29–31.

> You are my lamp, O Lord; the Lord turns my darkness into light. With your help I can advance against a troop with my God I can scale walls. As for God, his way is perfect; the word of the Lord is flawless. He is a shield for all who take refuge in him.
>
> Samuel 2: 29–31

I think I need a light and a shield to take refuge behind.

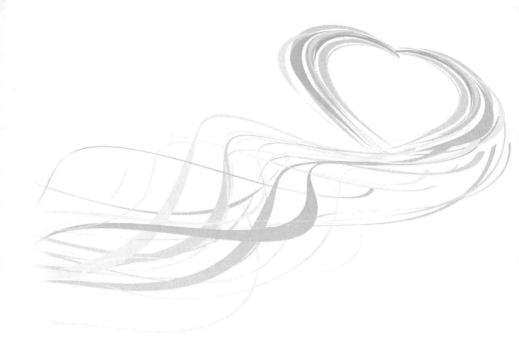

Visions

Wednesday, December 11, 2002
cold, light snow, twenty eight degrees

Last night, I dreamed of two snakes. These were very beautiful snakes. One was extremely large, at least twelve feet long. Both were full of colors. They were green, yellow, red, purple— all very vibrant colors. They displayed circles, triangles, and other prominent markings. The snakes slithered all around me on the floor and around my body. I was not terrified. I was intrigued by their beauty. I knew that, even though they were beautiful, they were evil. Could this be Satan in my life? Did this snake represent cancer in my body? I killed the larger one with all of the inner and physical strength that I could find. The smaller one moved away from me. I must save strength to kill the other when it returns.

Today, I met *the* doctor to be scheduled with if you have breast cancer in West Michigan. Doctor CS is a chemo doctor and a surgeon. That should be a comforting thought to many people. This is one person who understands both regimens and could coordinate them from one office. That certainly seems less complicated and would be an awesome thing. Because of this, scheduling an evaluation appointment soon was not available. My friend who knows this doctor personally was able to make my appointment for me. This doctor is local and could, after the clinical study is performed, do the surgery and the chemotherapy. That would save me from driving three hours one way to have treatments.

My appointment time was scheduled for five minutes, and she was one hour late. The conversation started with, "Hello, I am very busy every day, you have five minutes then I must break for lunch." The doctor then stated, "I am concerned about the size of the tumor." Understandable, I am also. She doesn't seem too concerned with *me*. She never once asked if I had any questions. Without explanation of the options available, she looked at me and asked, "What surgery, lumpectomy or mastectomy, would you like to have done? Do you want a sentinel node biopsy or all lymph nodes removed the day of surgery then biopsied?

I had done much research and had been to U of M but she had no idea of how much knowledge I had. I did know that having lymph nodes removed could cause many complications, but if they had cancer in them I definitely *did* want them removed.

Dr. CS gave no opinion or insight as to any complications. She didn't ask if I understood the treatment options. She checked her watch and looked at me again. I needed to decide if I wanted a lumpectomy or mastectomy. She offered no pros or cons to either. Dr CS did state that a cryo surgery clinical trial could be a big concern, making margins not clear of cancer. She had not ever participated in a clinical study such as this and didn't attend the University of Michigan. She really wasn't interested in participating in research at this time. If I wanted no clinical trial but I did want my breast removed and chemo with her, she would do that. Not that she *explained* any of the options.

I am sure that at this point I looked like a deer in headlights. Dr. CS seemed too busy for patients. If this was truly my choice and decision, I choose *no cancer. Poof!* My cancer was not gone.

My five-minute evaluation was finished, and so was she. My head was spinning. *Make a clear decision.* Will I choose a lumpectomy, which will leave a small, deformed breast with possible radiation and chemo, or a mastectomy, which leaves no breast, reconstruction, and possibly less radiation and chemo? The doctor had not offered statistics for each. I'm not afraid of dying, but I'm not walking into the grave either. Should I do this clinical study? Shall I help womankind or not?

I walked out of Dr. CS's office, realizing that she seemed to have too little time to explain the treatment that she would choose for me. I was again by myself. Tad was unavailable and too busy. I had the feeling like I had just been run over by a hit-and-run driver and left on the side of the road.

Writing will quiet my heart. I prayed to God; *please open my ears, eyes, and heart to see what choices that you have given me.* Wow. There are so many choices. I knew of a friend that had seen Dr. CS in the past. I called her tonight. She had gone to Dr. CS for a biopsy because my friend had heard how good she was. My friend said that after the procedure, the doctor's office left a detailed message on the home phone about her biopsy, which was positive. Her ten-year-old daughter was the first person to hear the message.

My friend immediately went to the University of Michigan, and had met Dr. Handsome. She valued the amount of empathy that he showed and his expertise. She was very happy to be alive and still feels that he was the answer for her prayers. The doctor took partial lymph nodes; and after months, she still has numbness but loves that doctor and the U of M facility. They would go there again. She and her husband said, "Don't rush the decision, and go with your gut feeling and good doctors." I asked God to help with this choice.

Thursday, December 12, 2002

Last night, I had a very graphic dream. I was in the operating room, prepared for surgery; and at my feet stood West Michigan's answer to breast cancer doctors. She looked like the evil witch from *The Wizard of Oz.* She just stood there with her broom and scary nose and face with a dark crooked hat. She stood there, cackling. "My pretty, it will be over soon."

Wow, God! Need you be so graphic? When I awoke, I picked up the phone and dialed the University of Michigan to set up surgery and the clinical study. I had no idea how I was going to get there and home, but I knew that was where God wanted me, and it was where I wanted to be. Somehow, he would help provide a person to go with me.

> If you make the most high your dwelling—even my Lord who is my refuge—then no harm will befall you, no disaster will come near your tent. For he will command his angels concerning you to guard you in all your ways; they will lift you up in their hands, so that you will not strike your foot against a stone. You will tread upon the lion and the cobra; you will trample the great lion and the serpent.
>
> Psalm 91:9–13

God's Gift to Me: Horses

very gray, mildly foggy, extremely damp, a little snow on the ground, forty six degrees

What a great day it was! This morning, at 10:36 a.m., it was very quiet. Nothing was moving and no dogs were barking. Everyone was at work, and the world was at a hush. I slowly walked out to the barn, feeling the cold dampness penetrating my skin. I brushed and felt Khanada's warm, fuzzy, white coat. She is always so responsive to what I need. This horse is 1,200 pounds of God's creation. She is a loving friend indeed. Khanada pushed against me and wanted to rub her head on me.

This was a day made by God for a peaceful ride. I tacked her up, and away we briskly trotted down the drive. Today, this road was reminiscent of a country road that I had ridden on daily when I had gone on a magnificent trip to Ireland. It was quiet; with absolutely no cars or vehicle noises, and Khanada didn't whinny or call for Laddie. No turning around at that point. Khanada was at a trot, faster and faster and faster. Then, at a canter, we were wild and free. She had one goal in mind—rhythmic, faster—and she was absolutely beautiful.

My job at this point was to hold steady and let her lead. It was a little like dancing. One has to lead, and so I gave the lead up to only follow. Usually I don't ride out by myself, especially in fog, but what could happen? At the worst, I could get killed. I already am full of cancer. I'll take my chances on this gorgeous mount. She felt so alive under me. I could feel the cold, damp air in my face. It was absolutely grand to be alive on this day. Thank you, God.

It is wonderful to live in the country and see God's creations every day that I choose to open my eyes. I love the wind, trees, animals, stars, rivers, and the flowers that grow where only dead leaves are now.

When I ride, it is the freest place on the earth to be. The movement and rhythm is mystical, magical, and haunting to my soul. It's as if I have wings to fly. I head back home and off to a late day at work with the Holy Spirit within me. I heard these words ringing in my ears: "then the trees of the forest will sing, they will sing for joy before the Lord, for he comes to judge the earth. Give thanks to the Lord for he is good." Chronicles 1 16:33–34

A Clinical Study: Cryosurgery

Tuesday, December 17, 2002
gloomy winter day in Michigan

My son, Matthew, arrived home from college yesterday; he is tired, but he wants to go to University of Michigan for this clinical study appointment with me. I told him that I could pick up his friend from the University of Michigan for Christmas break. Not wanting to have others perceive him as uncaring, Tad decided that he would also go.

This is the first day of any cancer treatment, a day that I have envisioned for what seems an eternity now. I do not know what to expect but I am feeling at ease in the Lord's arms. All of the decisions are made, and this is the first day to staying alive. I pray, *God, give me the strength to do these things to stay alive on your earth.* I don't want to leave my children.

At the University of Michigan, Tad and Matt went to find something to do. Tad was only there to be the driver for the appointment. I went to blood draws and other tests. I saw a lady my age; she was also a patient. I had seen her before. She was always with the same man. Could he be her husband? That man has stayed with her for every test that he could. Wow! I started to talk with her in the waiting area. She is my age and named Jane. Her husband, Ted, is with her. She also has two boys about my children's age and lives in Toledo. Talking, we found out that we also share coming from large families and we have the *same* birthday. I think we both are nervous about the unknown, but somehow, our friendship is instant. While waiting together for what seemed like hours, we talked about all the tests we had already been through. We shared with each other what kind of cancer we had been diagnosed with and how we had each discovered that we had cancer.

We discussed the great staff that we had met at the hospital and our families. We then had more blood draws for each of us and more waiting. These blood draws are part of the clinical study. My new friend, Jane, was whisked away by the friendly doctors for treatment as I waited and prayed that this was the correct decision. I waited and waited in the deafening silence alone.

I was next. Dr. Handsome entered with his welcoming and brilliant smile. Good. I felt comfortable with him as a person. The nurses were very nice, laughing and giggling. I think they like him too. My gown was taken off and breasts exposed yet again. Dr. Handsome said with a gorgeous smile, "Let's begin." Cancer is so humbling. There was a thin, needle-like argon gas probe that was inserted into the center of the tumor. This probe would freeze the tumor within a two centimeter area. To prevent frostbite in the live tissues, a syringe of saline solution was constantly being injected around the outside of the cancer site. This was like the Discovery Channel on my *own* body.

Dr. Handsome has kept us all entertained with information about Chicago and Ann Arbor restaurants. The time flew by. My husband and son were waiting for me. Matt showed concern on his face. He said, "Mom do you need help getting back into the car?" Then, when he saw that I appeared to be okay, a smile brightened his face; and he hugged me with warm, welcoming arms. Tad was stoic, non-emotional. No open arms there. He was the driver. Next, it was off to pick up Matt's friend from high school who is now attending the University of Michigan. It is the beginning of his Christmas break, and we can save his parents a trip by bringing him home tonight. On the way home, Tad offered to take us out for dinner. We were all starving, and it must have been that the whole world was also hungry. The wait was over one hour. Outside, it was snowing and snowing more. I had no Tylenol and was getting *very* sore. It felt like a lifetime until we got home.

My breast feels now, as I write late in the evening, like it has an ice ball in it. It is as hard as a rock. Boy, I pray that this clinical study helps save a life somewhere. My instructions were to take Tylenol if in pain and have no treatment for three weeks. I will return for blood draws and surgery in three weeks. It is late, and I have to work tomorrow. I will fall to sleep with my newest best friends: Tylenol and Tylenol.

Wednesday, December 18, 2002

On awaking, my chest felt as though it had been bludgeoned. I looked at my breast. It was completely black, blue, green, and yellow. If it were artwork, this might look great; but this was my breast, and it *hurt*. I was having extreme intermittent, piercing pain. I searched for my Tylenol. I went to work and called Dr. Handsome at the University of Michigan. He called back right away. He had other people from the clinical study calling today.

I explained the symptoms, and I explained that I was extremely black and blue. I told him, "I maybe won't have to keep the surgery date because I think this breast may just fall off." I mentioned, "When I have severe pain, I envision that these pains are warriors fighting the cancer off with spears, shields, and lots of armor."

He laughed and asked, "Can you send me a picture of your breast?" Since this study had not been done before, he wanted to see the bruising. Send a picture of my breast? Am I crazy? I guess so. I happened to have a Polaroid camera at work, so I went and took a few Polaroid snapshots of my "clinical breast" in the bathroom on my lunch hour. Then, like I knew what I was doing, I faxed them to the clinical study office to the head of the clinical study, a.k.a. Dr. Handsome. I am beginning to realize that having cancer will be very humbling.

Dr. Handsome called me in the evening to say, "When you sent the photos it was of great help for I could see how extensive the bruising was." It also helped him to view where the bruising was in relation to the placement of the argon gas probe. With this information, they would better understand how to keep the living tissues more alive during the treatment. My new best friend is Tylenol, and I am often envisioning many men with spears inside of me fighting against the cancer. I opened my Bible, and this text stared back at me:

> Therefore put on the full armor of God, so that when the day of evil comes, you may be able to stand your ground, and after you have done everything, to stand.
>
> Stand firm then, with the belt of truth buckled around your waist, with the breastplate of righteousness in place and with your feet fitted with the readiness that comes from the gospel of peace.
>
> In addition to all of this, take up the shield of faith, with which you can extinguish all the flaming arrows of the evil

one. Take the helmet of salvation and the sword of the Spirit, which is the word of God. And pray in the Spirit on all occasions with all kinds of prayers and requests. With this in mind, be alert and always keep on praying for all the saints.

Ephesians 6:13–18

I now visualize Warriors in my body doing battle with the evil one, and I am now equipped to do battle with God by my side. Oh God, you are amazing.

Here We Go

Sunday, January 5, 2003
very gloomy, low hanging clouds, dark, cold

Tad has become more distant and very detached from me and our family. He comes home later than usual and is never in a good mood anymore. I can't get him to smile or laugh. When I suggest doing something such as a walk or drive, he is no longer interested like he used to be. In him, I see hour after hour of a long, unhappy face. He never asks about treatment or if he can accompany me to an appointment. He no longer asks how my parents are doing. He no longer talks much to the children or attends any of their events. He goes to basketball games by himself, not wanting family as company. He is wanting, very much so, to be a loner. I tried to talk with him, and a counselor has offered to speak with him; but he has no interest.

Monday, January 6, 2003

Today was very busy. I had to work, run errands, and be prepared for surgery tomorrow at the University of Michigan. The choice has been made: lumpectomy and sentinel node biopsy at the University of Michigan and chemotherapy and radiation at Holland, within miles of home and work.

Jonathan, our pastor, came to our home for support and prayer before leaving tomorrow for the University of Michigan. I like Jonathan. I find his voice very comforting. He choose Psalm 139 to read to me. This will be my healing Psalm. For me, this entire Psalm is extremely powerful; but today I find these words from this psalm so comforting:

> O Lord you have searched me and you know me. You know when I sit and when I rise; you perceive my thoughts from afar. You discern my going out and my lying down; you are familiar with all of my ways. Before a word is on my tongue you know it completely O Lord.
>
> If I go up into heaven you are there; if I make my bed in the depths you are there. If I rise on the wings of the dawn, if I settle on the far side of the sea, even there your hand will guide me your right hand will hold me fast.
>
> Psalm 139: 1–4, 8–10

Laurelin and Travis came and stayed close to me while our pastor read the complete psalm to us. Tad chose to stand by himself in the other room. They all looked somewhat anxious, but I really felt a deep peace in my heart and soul. I have the best family, friends, best doctors, and God with me at the head of it all. How could I feel anxious?

I walked out to the barn at 10:30 or 11:00 p.m. Those furry horses with their winter coats are so warm. They are extremely perceptive when something is different with me or when I am upset. They both walked near and sensed that something is wrong or different, and they wrapped their bodies around mine and entwined me. They smelled good and were so warm.

As I walked home, the stars were very bright, like little candles to light the way. God is incredibly good to me. These stars are like millions of little night lights for my pleasure and safety. It was very cold. Orion's belt was above the barn. On the way back home the dogs, Pumpkin and Pollix, took pleasure in the cold, crisp air. They always enjoyed the walk to the barn and back home. Tonight, there was fresh snow to roll and roll in. When we arrived at home everyone was in bed. It was quiet, and I enjoyed it. The Christmas tree lights this year are the most beautiful I ever remember. Am I now looking differently and enjoying each part of life like my first breath ever or my last? Now as I write the room is warm and radiant. The cats are asleep under the Christmas tree. My dogs are at my feet. Tad and Laurelin also are at rest; and hopefully, Matt is resting at college.

Tomorrow, I will be leaving for surgery at the University of Michigan. Tad has said that he will drive and stay with me while I have surgery. I pray that this is true. He has abandoned me before.

It was in Europe about twelve years ago on the trip of a lifetime when we were with Tad's brother and wife. Tad had taken from my purse all of my travelers checks on the plane, stating, "Someone could easily steal your entire purse, and all of your money would be lost. I will return them when we are safe in a car."

The four of us, tired and excited, traveled in the car to Belgium from the Netherlands. We stopped in a town to sightsee for a while and shop. I had asked Tad for my traveler's checks; and he said, "When you want to purchase something I will give them to you." I protested because he had a knack for disappearing at the most inconvenient times. My protest went in vain as he walked off to the store to shop. We were together for maybe five minutes. I turned around to ask for my checks to purchase something, and he could not be found.

The other couple had left for their own adventures the minute that Tad locked the car doors. Now I stood in a shop in Belgium with no money, no car keys, no phone, no husband, and not being able to speak one word of the language. I returned to the car numerous times in the next hours that passed.

I searched shops, buildings, churches, parks, and alleys to no avail, looking for Tad. In a coffee shop, the man asked if I wanted coffee; and I showed him that I had no money. He was extremely kind and offered me a biscotti and a cup of coffee. Hours and hours later, Tad showed up at the car as I was again waiting for him. He, of course, was upset at me and couldn't understand why I would have been the least bit inconvenienced for the last six hours. I explained that this wasn't normal behavior for him or anyone and I would not tolerate it again.

History could never repeat itself again. Or could it? He is my husband. If he said that he would be there for me as a driver and at my surgery time as my advocate, I had to trust that he would. I will need a support person for decisions during treatment and as support before and after surgery. I will not be able to drive myself home the three hours it would take, so he will be the driver. He has promised to be by my side.

I opened the Bible and prayed to God that this was the correct course. I read my favorite and most comforting psalm: Psalm 23. I turned pages to others verses that also touched my heart and calmed my soul.

> The Lord is my shepherd, I shall lack nothing. He makes me lie down in green pastures, he leads me beside quiet waters, he restores my soul. He guides me in paths of righteousness for his name's sake. Even though I walk through the valley of the shadow of death, I fear no evil, for you are with me; your rod and your staff, they comfort me. You prepare a

table before me in the presence of my enemies. You anoint my head with oil; my cup overflows. Surely goodness and love will follow me all the days of my life, and I will dwell in the house of the Lord forever.

Psalm 23

I sought the Lord and he answered me; he delivered me from all my fears. Those who look to him are radiant; their faces never covered with shame. This poor man called, and the Lord heard him; he saved him from out of all his troubles. The angel of the Lord encamps around those who fear him, and he delivers them. Taste and see that the Lord is good; Blessed is the man who takes refuge in him. Fear the Lord you his saints, for those who fear him lack nothing. The lions may grow weak and hungry, but those who seek the Lord lack no good thing.

Psalm 34: 4–10

For you created my inmost being; you knit me together in my mother's womb. I praise you because I am fearfully and wonderfully made; your works are wonderful, I know that full well. My frame was not hidden from you when I was made in the secret place. When I was woven together in the depths of the earth, your eyes saw my unformed body. All the days ordained for me were written in your book before one of them came to be.

Psalm 139: 13–16

Life, being alive on this earth is good.

Where Is My Advocate?

Tuesday, January 7, 2003
cloudy and gray today, a bitter chill in the air, twenty nine degrees,

I am up very early, and it is extremely difficult to write without my glasses on. Laurelin and I had a great breakfast and then she was off to school. We shared so many hugs, kisses, tears and I love you's. Tad said he would come to surgery with me today at the University of Michigan. We left at 7:45 a.m. and arrived on clear roads at 10:10 a.m. We shared no conversation after twenty-seven years of marriage. I heard only deafening silence. I can't share my thoughts with my husband of twenty-seven-plus years. I find this extremely sad.

The staff was very kind and helpful there, willing to answer questions and help in any way. Nan, the ultrasound nurse, greeted us in the waiting area, tan and with a smile. She just spent the last three weeks in the Dominican Republic. I have spent it thinking that there are warriors fighting against cancer in my breast, and when the fighting gets intense, it is Tylenol, Tylenol, Tylenol, and massive prayers. Then it was off to ultrasound and a new health history. Tad went to read somewhere. I was on my own.

I had run into Jane and her husband all day in tests. We had visited and shared many things considering I didn't know her at all before cancer. Ted, her husband, is a sailor on a Great Lakes boat and has been for years. This is a time of year that they sometimes get laid off due to tremendous storms on the Great Lakes. He has been with Jane by her side to wait at every test that we've had. Tad is somewhere. I haven't seen him all day.

4:00 p.m. Nuclear Medicine

This portion of the hospital was a sad place with many curtained areas. Behind the opened curtains I could see patients waiting for their next treatment. This was such an emotional place. There were many people with no hair; a large number of them being children. They look exhausted and wasted with no emotions, no laughter, very little life left inside. Their families looked the same. Will I be like that someday? It is okay to be tired and exhausted, but why not live until you die? I smiled at these people as I walk past and was greeted with one faint smile after another. Someday that may be me, and I pray that someone would give me a smile of hope and life.

For this procedure, I had two doctors. I realized this must be a serious, complicated medical procedure. The doctors here are always so young and handsome, and the women are all attractive. I asked how long they had been doing this job. Most of them answer about seven years since completing ten-plus years of school. Thank God that they devoted that much of their lives to save mine.

I asked the doctor of nuclear medicine, "How do you do this procedure? No one will tell me except that it is with nuclear medicine. But how do you get it into me? Does it hurt?"

The female doctor said, "It hurts a lot. Don't let anybody tell you it doesn't."

Okay. That is clear. It can't be any worse than cortisone injected into my elbow or having two children with no anesthetic. Could it?

Wow. It really did hurt. I am glad that they prepared me. Not worse, but somehow the initial gain doesn't seem as great as when you have a child. Long-term it will be wonderful. I saw Jane as I was leaving and she was going in. She looked concerned and asked, "How difficult was it?" I looked at her and smiled and said, "Piece of cake. Ask the nurses how they do the procedure. I'm still alive and kicking."

I was tired. I had a long day today and I have surgery tomorrow. Tad came and picked me up at 5:30 p.m. because this portion of the hospital closes at this time. These workers face life and death every day, and they pack up their lives here every night to go home and have a normal life for a few hours.

Tad took me out to an old favorite restaurant of ours from twenty-five years ago for dinner, The Gandy Dancer. It is still a beautiful place for dinner. What a great treat. We did not have much conversation; there are many thoughts rushing through my mind. Tad is extremely quiet. He says he can't hold or hug me, can't kiss me, and can't talk about it. Why am I facing cancer surgery with someone who would rather be elsewhere?

We went back to our hotel room, and I tried to locate my Bible. I opened to this verse:

"I lift up my eyes to the hills. Where does my help come from? My help comes from the Lord, the maker of heaven and earth."

Psalm 121: 1–2

In the morning, I will read this entire Psalm again and receive strength from it. I will rest for now.

Are We Having Fun Yet?

Wednesday, January 8, 2003
another gray day, cold, damp, old dirty snow

I am up early. I slept pretty good, considering that this is surgery day. We were at the hospital by 7:45 a.m. Tad left the surgical area to go read at the cafeteria. He knew that after tests this morning, my surgery may be moved up as much as three or four hours earlier in the day. Tad said he would check back at the surgery station periodically, and he had a phone that we could call if the time was changed. He went somewhere to read a book by himself.

Now it was solo for me to nuclear medicine again, this time to track the radioactive isotope with x-rays. I saw Jane returning from x-ray, and she, with a broad smile, said, "Piece of cake." Then I was escorted off to have a wire inserted in my right breast, just like a normal day.

The nurses seem to think that it was easier to locate the center of the tumor due to the cryo surgery. I thought these women doctors and nurses realized that it was a humbling experience to have this procedure done. They were very patient. It was a bit like playing battleship on my breast. They had a grid with coordinates. I stood very still with my breast against the marked, clear, glass grid.

They used mammograms and ultrasound to find the center of the tumor, all the time calling out numbers that corresponded to the grid. This can take minutes or hours. When the center of the tumor is found, a twelve-inch-long metal wire is inserted into the exact center of the tumor for easier location during surgery. The extra length, or "tail", which is maybe six to nine inches long, is taped down to your skin so that it is not dislodged before surgery. I was let go early due to the fact that it went so well. Are we having fun yet?

At 10:00 a.m., I was in my hospital gown, which was falling open constantly in the rear area. I was told that surgery was moved to one and a half hours away rather than five hours. We were told earlier that this might happen. I had no cell phone; but Tad did, and he knew that the surgery time might be changed to a much earlier hour.

Still wearing my fashionable hospital gown, I tried to call him from a pay phone that I had located in the hospital. I left two messages. Now I was getting aggravated and feeling upset because it had been quite some time now and Tad had not returned even one call. His last words as he left in the morning were, "Just call and I'll be right there for you."

The nurse suggested that I double gown—one in front and one in back so my back side was not exposed. Great idea! Now this is a fashion statement. I seemed to be the only new trendsetter in the entire hospital. I set out on a quest to find my husband. Maybe he would be in the hospital cafeteria. Did I mention that I am walking around with a wire inserted in my breast and taped to my skin, wearing only a double hospital gown and surgical boots?

I have been in this area of the hospital enough in the past weeks to know many of the nurses that I pass by name. The nurses were at their various stations; and they asked, "Have you lost something?" I'm thinking maybe my *mind*. Thank God no one had a camera. I explained that it was my husband that I was looking for. They said they would keep watch and send him down to surgery if they saw him.

Finally, after a half hour of walking and calling from desks and pay phones to Tad's cell, I reached the cafeteria. The wonderful aromas slowly entered my nostrils and worked their way to my brain. I was starving.

If I needed a doctor or nurse, this is where I should come. There were hundreds of them there. They were trying to act like a patient in double hospital gowns and booties was a regular site in the cafeteria. Tad was nowhere to be seen, and he was not returning any messages. Frustrated, I quit. I returned to the surgery area and waited for my surgery hour alone.

I was prepared and ready to go for surgery, but had no husband. My friend Jane was laughing and joking with me as we waited in the pre-operating room area. We didn't want the nurses to get us mixed up. We had the same birthday, same cancer, we both did the same clinical trial, had the same surgeon, and we weigh about the same. The important note is that our cancers were on the opposite sides, so we had notes written on our chests and arms: this is the correct side for surgery.

We got everyone's attention. The nurses and doctors were hooting with laughter and referred to us as the twins. Jane was taken in first for her surgery. Ted, her loving husband, gave her a kiss and a reassuring hug and said, "I love you. I will be here when you wake up." She flashed a beautiful smile. I said a prayer for her and Ted.

God truly is the only one who knows where my husband Tad was. He knew that the surgery time might be changed. It seemed that he would have left his cell phone on. He could also have checked back with me or the surgery desk at least every few hours, for Pete's sake. He had a phone. I didn't! A half hour before surgery, he showed up. I was upset but happy that he was there. I wouldn't have to face this alone. My loving and caring husband would be by my side when I was pushed into the surgical suite.

When Tad arrived, he was instructed, by the nurses that were calling him on the phone and leaving messages just minutes ago, to sit and wait for the doctor. The doctor would very soon finish surgery on my friend Jane, and it would be my turn. The nurse told Tad, "The doctor will be out very soon to talk with you about your wife's surgery."

Surgery would be happening within a half hour. Tad didn't sit. He left the hospital! A half hour later, and the nurses had called Tad at least fifteen to twenty times. No answer and they had left many messages. The doctors didn't want to do a surgery without next of kin or guardian there during surgery. This person was to make any decisions that may need to be made during surgery.

My doctor, the head surgeon of the oncology department, was ready to perform my surgery. We were still waiting for my advocate to show up. I had waited for over four weeks to have this doctor do this surgery. I was sitting with an IV in my arm. I had given blood samples. I now had a wire inserted inside my breast. I had radioactive dye that was injected into my breast floating in my body, and I had undergone a clinical study where I had my breast tumor frozen. I have done all of these things to get to this day and now this day is actually here. Where is Tad, where is my advocate? His only part in all of this was to drive the car and be here when I went into surgery, where is he?

Tad had left the surgical area, and he couldn't be located. Surgery wouldn't be performed without an advocate present. I felt completely abandoned, tossed out, left at the side of the road with nothing. My new friend, Ted, was coming out of surgery with Jane; and I asked him if he could be my advocate. I explained why I needed an advocate. He said with a broad smile, "Sure." After all, he just did this with his wife. The only thing that we really knew about each other was that his wife and I had extremely similar cancers and we both had two children.

I gave my Mom and Dad's phone number in Florida to a nurse. The nurse then took my beautiful beaded bracelet off of my wrist. My coworkers had lovingly made this bracelet for me to say "Good luck, and good-riddance, cancer!" Each of them had selected or made a special bead or charm that reminded them of me. When revealed at a party that my coworkers had for me, the stories of why each piece had been chosen had brought tears to my eyes.

I had not yet let the nurses take it off of me, thinking that Tad would be back any minute to remove it and keep it safe until I awoke after surgery. The nurse promised that I would get it back and that she would personally care for it.

I was alone, facing cancer surgery; but I realized that I am not alone. I had great nurses and doctors with an abundance of compassion. I had my new friends, Jane and Ted. The most important thing to remember was I had God, who promised to show me the way and never leave me. A prayer from my doctor, and the eyeglasses were removed—mine, fortunately, not his. Away I went to have surgery. I only remember many people, lots of lights, and a joyful, peaceful feeling that God was with me.

Hours later, I awoke. Wow. I had a little trouble coming out of the anesthetic; and the first thing that I noticed was that my good luck bracelet was on my wrist and Tad's face was looking down at me. It was good to see him. Where had he been?

Hours later, they said that I was doing so well that we could go home and not have to stay through the night. I was thinking that a three-plus-hour ride in a car to get home didn't sound good. I wished I could stay. Jane looked great fifteen minutes after surgery. What was with me?

The ride home was like a beautiful dream. The weather was a warm fifty-six degrees on January 8 in Michigan. There was a breathtaking sunset. God was saying, "I am here. I am with you." The thought ran through my head that it was the most spectacular sunset that I had ever seen, and we were driving straight into it. This was a gift from God for me and anyone else that stopped for a moment to gaze at God's glory. How could I be that important?

> Praise the Lord. Praise the Lord, O my soul. I will praise the Lord all of my life; I will sing praise to my God as long as I live. Do not put trust in the princes, in mortal men, who cannot save. When their spirit departs, they return to the ground; on that day their plans come to nothing. Blessed is he whose help is the God of Jacob, whose hope is in the Lord his God, the Maker of heaven and earth, the sea, and everything in them—the Lord who remains faithful forever.
> Psalm 146: 1–6

Is There Life after Surgery?

Thursday, January 9, 2003
cold, overcast, twenty four degrees

I am not too tired and not too sore. I have taken my pain medicine and last night I slept in my own bed. I'm really feeling irritable. I'm on my own. Tad is back at work. I asked him where he had gone during surgery. He explained that he had left to check out of the hotel room. How convenient that it was right at surgery time. Will he ever have any idea how many people he inconvenienced with that?

I have received many wonderful cards, and Laurelin is trying so hard to help me. This morning friends have been bringing meals. How wonderful. There has been much visiting and I tried to pick up a few things around the house and check my e-mails. Now I'm tired. Is this too much activity for the first day?

It is later in the day and I'm tired. I am very tired and rather sore. I have had greater pain than this, but it doesn't make it any easier. My chest is encompassed in bandages. I took Laurelin to Travis's house to catch a ride to go view Travis's swim meet. Then I came home and lay down for ten minutes, and that became three hours. I woke up for ten minutes; slept two hours then showered and closed my eyes again.

I ate and shut my eyes for ten minutes and awoke in the morning. Is this life when you are healing?

Friday, January 10, 2003

Yesterday I did check my e-mails. I had a great one from my friend Jane. She seems like such a nice lady. How could our paths cross and we become good friends because of cancer? We joked on the phone and giggled about the yet another fashion statement that we shared. We both wore a post-surgical colorful tube top. This is a style straight from the 1960s fashion magazines. This top holds all of our bandages in place while we are healing. I am sporting blue and green daisies on my tube top. Green and blue are both healing colors.

Today I got cleaned up as much as possible by myself. I thought that I felt good enough to take CPR class. This class was being offered at my dental office today. This is mandatory yearly to renew my dental hygienist license. Our entire office will be together today in this training and if I don't take it today I will have to find another time and place, so I will go today. Is my brain screwed on backward that I thought that I should do this? I was so extremely tired when I got home. I slept, ate, and slept again.

Saturday, January 11, 2003
cold, no wind

I think of Jane. Did our paths cross only because we both had an aggressive cancer? Only God will know. Now big soft snow-flakes are falling outside. They are so beautiful, and each one is unique. The issue of getting rid of the horses has come up again, even though I have been working my regular schedule. Tad is still looking at buying new golf clubs, and the expense of the country club is never brought up.

Today, I called Dr. Rubie (my horse vet and dear friend) and asked, "What do you know about the Chef Center, other than it is a home for older retired horses?" Dr. Rubies' comment was, "Thais, the horses are used in treatment for the mentally and physically handicapped. The horses must not spook if a wheelchair and bouncing balls are present. The horses are well taken care of until they pass away."

I called the Chef Center today. My horses are too tall for what they want—not to mention that I would have to work on the bouncing ball and wheelchair thing. Giving them away might kill me if the cancer doesn't. They give me more support on a daily basis than my husband.

Sunday, January 12, 2003
sunny, cold, seventeen degrees

I yawned all through church like I hadn't had enough sleep. When I arrived home from church I had a short nap, changed clothes and went to the barn. Tad is gone. He just left—no note, no explanation. I napped again and made dinner. My very dear friend Shari brought dinner for tomorrow. I'm exhausted.

Monday, January 13, 2003
bright sunshine, sixteen degrees

I am off work today. My doctor at the University of Michigan has suggested that I take off six weeks of work. Is he kidding? I have to get back to work. I will take off a vacation day or two.

It is so nice to have complete quiet to myself. The entire morning consisted of cleaning a few cupboards. I move so slowly these days, but at least I am still moving. I have received many wonderful cards from friends and family. What have I done to deserve so many wonderful people in my life? I went to play with the horses. It is wonderful to have them in my backyard, with the neighbors taking care of them. It is the neighbor's barn, but Laddie and Khanada are so close.

Tuesday, January 14, 2003

Today, I worked a shorter day, from about 7:30 a.m. to 2:00 p.m. My dear friend, Shari, came in to cover my afternoon at work. I came home and crashed by 3:00 p.m. and woke up by 5:30 p.m. I'm incredibly tired. Walking to the barn in the evening to see Laddie and Khanada, did make me feel much more energized.

The sky was bright with a million twinkling stars. These look like God's candles in the night, lighting the way as I walk through life, placed there in the heavens for me to view and enjoy with a full moon. God is always there for me. He has to keep reminding me of this over and over. When will I learn? I am so at peace. Just think, if I hadn't taken a walk in the moonlight to the barn, I would not have seen all of this great display of grandeur. God has once again reminded of His grace.

Wednesday, January 15, 2003
very cold, snow and lots of it

Today, I will go to work late and return much later. As I walked to the barn in the morning, I saw that the snow had fallen and accumulated at least four inches of awesome fluffy powder. Pollix, my Nova Scotia Duck Toller, was in all his glory rolling, rolling, and rolling. He looked up at me, all a glistening white, sneezing and loving God's earth. Pumpkin, the collie, was taking notes from Pollix and was learning very fast. They were making snowballs with their noses. Watching the animals play brings to me laughter and bountiful joy.

It was so cold, and this would have been great snow skiing powder if I hadn't had bandages wrapping my entire chest. Even the horses are playing their own game of fox and goose, cut the pie, rearing and running and head-tossing with muzzles full of snow. Today, the world is playful; and I am grateful to be alive.

I came home and called my doctor to see if the biopsy had been completed. It had been finished; but my doctor was not in, and the nurse was not giving out any information. She told me that he would be calling me soon. I was again to wait. I think I have been here before. He will call back with the results of the lymph node biopsy. At that time, the answer to my questions will be given. Is there cancer in the lymph nodes? Is there a small amount of cancer or a large amount? But I am guessing that the news will not be *no* cancer. Tad is gone again tonight. Tad said that it was buddies' card night. Maybe he will be more normal after a night out. Healing is taking all of my strength now.

Thursday, January 16, 2003

This morning, at 3:30 a.m., I woke up from a deep sleep and couldn't go back to sleep. This is the day I should find out about the biopsy. As I write, I have a feeling this may not be good news; yet I know that I have to face this, whatever it is. In the bedroom, there is a large window with a seat long enough to sleep on. I lay down and viewed the brightest moon. It seemed as though it was my only friend at the moment; and it stared back at me and seemed to whisper echoes of, *I am with you.* I felt more at peace being showered in God's light and finally went back to sleep.

p.m.

My surgeon from U of M called in the early evening and clearly stated with a kind, caring voice, "*Yes,* Thais. You have cancer in many lymph nodes and actually need the complete axillary node area removed."

I now know that the cancer has spread and this will be another major surgery. Tad is not home. I have no one to talk this over with. I will have surgery on February 5. That day is my Dad's birthday. He is in Florida with Mom, trying to recover from his stroke. This is not good news to tell him because I fear that it will deteriorate his health more. Tad is not available to talk with me; and when he came home, he retreated to his chair and didn't want to hear about it. So much for the vows we took at our wedding, "In *sickness* and in *health.*"

My gut flips, and my mind is going in circles as if a hurricane is beginning. My husband just said, "I don't want to hear about it." This is the one person that I have shared my entire life with. This feels like a category 10 hurricane. I am by *myself,* trying to find shelter *anywhere.*

God Sees My Need through a Friend

Monday, January 20, 2003
cloudy, cold, damp winter day

This morning I was at work, still in shock that I have to have another surgery; the worst part is that I have cancer that has spread into my lymph nodes. This is really not a good thing. I was trying to keep my cool even though my body was still wrapped like a mummy with bandages. Even the thought of my flowery blue and green tube top that was hiding under my work smock wasn't bringing a smile to my face.

It had been suggested, by my doctors, to take at least three to six weeks off after my last surgery, but I have taken a day or two off. Tad has shown concern that if I take more time off without pay I may not be able to pay the bills that he has assigned to me. If that happens, the first things to go are my horses. I pay very little for the two of them. Maybe he could take one less trip with the guys or cut back on the country club or play fewer cards? That would help.

Each day, as I work, I am sharing small details with my patients and friends as they ask what is happening in my life. It has been as if I am in a complete daze, almost surreal. I feel as if I am experiencing work, treatment, and life from outside of my body. My family, friends, patients and co-workers have been a wonderful support to me. They are my own cheering squad, there to cheer me on day after day.

I feel so little support from Tad. I suppose that it is good that I am working even though my exhaustion is complete.

Just as I was having these thoughts of loneliness, my next patient on this day of work arrived at the front window of the dental office that I work in. This patient is a caring, God-fearing, beautiful African-American woman. She is about my age. Somehow this woman has raised five children mostly by herself; and they are all wonderful, polite, gracious, grown children, an accomplishment that any mother would be proud of. She has done this as a single parent, with support and with the grace of God. I find this exceptional.

Sandra is a beautiful woman on the outside, but she glows of the Holy Spirit from the inside. I can call this woman a friend. We talked about kids, work and, of course, teeth because that was why she had made the appointment. But she noticed that something about me was different and asked, "Are you all right?" In my mind, I was trying to figure how I would tell her that I had an aggressive cancer. How could I say that I had already had one surgery and would be having another in a short period to remove more cancer?

So I just blurted it out in three simple words that summed it all up, "I have *cancer*."

She leaped up out of the chair and in one big swoop grabbed me up and gave me a fantastic bear hug. This was just what I needed.

At that moment, she took away all my emotional pain and asked if she could pray with me. We discussed all of the treatment that would be done and some of the anxiety that goes along with this.

I said, "At this time, I know that I have cancer that has spread to my lymph nodes. I just don't know how much cancer there is."

She asked, "Do you have support for this journey?"

I explained that family and friends had been wonderful.

Sandra came closer and looked into my eyes when she asked, "What about your husband?"

"Sandra, he is very distant and not available for emotional or physical comfort."

"Thais, I will pray for your family each day."

Sandra said that two weeks ago, while watching the Oprah show, she had seen an interview of a woman who had gone through treatments for breast cancer. This woman had spoken about her journey through the treatments and what she felt that she had to do in her life for changes and treatment. When Sandra was in the bookstore days before this dental appointment she saw the book this woman had written. Sandra had been moved to purchase the book and began to read it that very day. All she could think was; *I don't even know anyone with cancer! Why did I buy this book?* Sandra was now there with me, sharing her story about this cancer book she had bought. We just looked at each other; and she said, "Thais, God had me buy that book for you!"

With tears in her eyes, she went to the car to get the book for me. Today, when she gave me the gift of that book, I asked, "Will you sign in it for me, please?"

God had already signed it by orchestrating that it was in my hand at that moment.

We both showered great tears of joy over big bear hugs and praises to God. Thank goodness it was lunch and the other patients were gone. We stood and cried. We both laughed at how God works even when we don't know it. And we prayed together.

> My commandment is this: Love each other as I have loved you.
>
> John 15:12

Sandra has made my life much more complete today, and I am much richer in the Holy Spirit because of this friend. Yes, God, I know that you are there. Thank you for reminding me of this. Thank you for bringing into the path I am walking a dear friend of yours and mine.

Sandra returned later with soft caps for my head, to wear when my hair fell out. They are stylish and colorful, and I will be proud to wear them.

At night, as I opened my Bible, I turned to Colossians.

> My purpose is that they may be encouraged in heart and united in love, so that they may have the full riches of complete understanding, in order that they may know the mystery of God, namely Christ in whom are hidden all the treasures of wisdom and knowledge.
>
> Colossians 2:2

I will fall to sleep thanking God for these little miracles that he performs in my life each day. I will thank him for sending me very wonderful friends.

Sunshine State Here I Come

Thursday, January 30, 2003
warm, warm, warm, seventy eight degrees

Wow. I can feel the balmy moisture in the air as I step outside of the airport. Everything is moving, and people are everywhere. It is *season* in West Palm Beach Florida, and the best part is that I am here. Erin, my level-headed sister, best friend, and advisor picked me up; and it was early in the day as we headed off to lunch in Lake Worth, where she lives all year long.

I recently had all of the bandages removed from my chest. I am healing and gaining strength for my next surgery. I wanted to come down and see Mom, Dad, Erin, and her husband, Bo. I will also stop and visit with my friend Dawn in Wellington, Florida before the next major surgery.

Erin and Bo have a beautiful bed and breakfast in Lake Worth, which is a huge amount of daily work; yet, they are always so kind to open their home to me. This afternoon I rested by the pool for a while. I'm exhausted physically and mentally. I had asked Tad if he would come with me. Tad was not interested in coming. He is too busy. Too busy doing what?

I had a wonderful dinner with Mom, Dad, Erin, and Bo. Mom and Dad are both exhausted with physical therapy, doctor's appointments, and the stresses of not feeling well. It has all taken its toll on them, never knowing the outcome of all this running and doctoring on a day-to-day basis. My Dad wants to know why he just can't take this cancer from me and meet his Father in heaven.

The night was warm, and there was a gentle breeze. I know that it was God softly caressing each one of my family members at the evening dinner on the patio, complete with candles and soft music. There was great laughter and, at times, sudden tears. God, thank you for this opportunity to be with family that loves me so greatly. Tad was too busy to come on a trip with me. He is constantly promising a trip together, but everything seems to get in the way.

Friday, January 31, 2003
warm Florida sunshine, light breezes, seventy five degrees

My friend Dawn from Michigan, who now lives in Wellington, Florida, about twenty minutes from Erin, came today to take me to see the International Horse Show. Dawn has a heart of gold when it comes to others, and she is constantly my spiritual confidant. Her husband recently passed away (from many complications), and she is now on her own and making a good way of it. She knew everyone at the show, and the horses were beautiful. I am still incredibly sore where all of the stitches are still healing.

After the show, we went to visit friends with horses, so many great horses. I even got to ride Dawn's horse. This horse is a young, beautiful German Oldenburg. She is extremely athletic and very flexible. Her name is C'est La Vie, and she is very much a lady. She is the color of charcoal with what looks like white snowflakes that have randomly fallen on the soft gray. She is a princess.

I tried nothing too exciting for me today in the riding arena. I am still healing. A walk on this horse felt like heaven to me. What a beauty! Her gaits were soft, large, and fluid. It was such a gift for me to play with such a wonderful animal. After a great dinner, Dawn gave me a journal. The entire cover is the painting by Monet of the gardens at Givenchy. This painting has always inspired me. Dawn said, "This journal is to write in about the journey you have begun through cancer treatments with God by your side. Thais, you will be able to write each day and remember all of the good that God bestows on you."

"Dawn, this book will make me remember each day that God is with me, no matter how easy or difficult the day was. I will write it down each day to remember."

This day has been great fun. I feel young again, and I feel as though I move more effortlessly through my daily pain. Again, dear God, I am grateful to be alive. Wonderful friends and horses are always a great diversion for me. You always supply what I need to heal.

I think of the words that Dawn said about writing the gifts of God down, and I open my Bible.

> A wise man's heart guides his mouth, and his lips promote instruction. Pleasant words are a honeycomb, sweet to the soul and healing to the bones.
>
> Psalm 16:23–24

> Then your light will break forth like the dawn, and your healing will quickly appear; then your righteousness will go before you, and the glory of the Lord will be your rear guard. Then you will call, and the Lord will answer; you will cry for help, and he will say: Here am I.
>
> Isaiah 58:8–9

Off to the University of Michigan Again

Monday, February 3, 2003
eighty degrees

I am leaving sunshine. My birthday is today. I turned forty-eight years old. I left Florida today to come home to Michigan for my third surgery. It will be on February 5, my father's birthday. This surgery will hopefully be my last. The doctors already know that I have an aggressive cancer.

The cancer has spread to the lymph nodes. The question is how many lymph nodes? This is not a good thing at all, and I haven't concerned anyone with this because I am strong. Truly, I am scared to death of knowing how much of the cancer is in my lymph nodes. My father is fighting his own battle. He is trying, through daily physical therapy and exercises, to regain use of his right side after his stroke.

Healing for him has been extremely slow, and it has been difficult for Mom also with having to see Dad not as himself. My prayer to God is, "Please don't let me die on my father's birthday." The airline captain found out somehow that it was my birthday. He arranged a first-class seat and a free chance to get into the sky lounge while I had a long and tedious layover. What a kind thing for the captain do to. Truly, God just keeps giving me gifts in this wilderness that I seem to be residing in now. This gave me a chance to be wined and dined in first class and quiet time to think about how much my family loves me.

I am beginning to realize more each day how rich life is with God. My family and friends only improve more each day. God, you work in wonderful and mysterious ways.

Tuesday, February 4, 2003
very gloomy Michigan day: no sun, no snow—only cold

Tad has promised, "I will stay with you for the surgery." He has decided to drive me the three-plus hours and stay overnight at the University of Michigan for my surgery tomorrow. This is a major surgery. They will remove all of the lymph nodes under my right arm. The doctors already know that more than three nodes have cancer.

Now I know that the cancer has spread away from the original site. They will take all the nodes and biopsy them to see how many have cancer. The incision will be about six inches long and could complicate the nerve endings in my hands to the point where I could have no or little feeling in my hands. I am a dental hygienist. Now *that* could be bad for working.

Tad is in his own world. I have been brave as much as possible by myself, facing so much of this without Tad's support. In the hotel room, I moved toward Tad, scared to death about this, another surgery. All the way to Ann Arbor, I had been praying, *Tad, please hold me close and tell me that you love me and that you will be there for me.* In the hotel room, my arms reached out to hold him. He drew away and threw his hands into the air. With a look of terror on his face, he said, "I cannot hug you!" No other explanation, just a statement of four words. How can four words have such an impact, four simple words?

The tears at first numbed my cheeks, and then my entire body was lifeless, without sensation, deadened, as if my entire body had received a large dose of anesthesia. The pain was so deep that I couldn't feel it.

As I went to bed, I held tightly my Bible and said many prayers. When I opened my Bible, I read these words.

> Humble yourselves, therefore, under God's mighty hand, that he may lift you up in due time. Cast all your anxieties on him because he cares for you. Be self controlled and alert. Your enemy the devil prowls around like a roaring lion looking for someone to devour. Resist him, standing firm in the faith, because you know that your brothers throughout the world are undergoing the same kind of sufferings. And the God of all grace, who called you to his eternal glory in Christ, after you have suffered a little while, will himself restore you and make you strong, firm and steadfast. To him be the power forever and ever. Amen.
>
> 1 Peter 5:6–11

Wednesday, February 5, 2003

Today is my Father's birthday and my surgery day. I have tried to be so strong and rely only on God; but truthfully, I really need a human hug and a kind human voice to say, "I'm here with you."

As Tad and I started out our day together in the hotel room, I said, "Please hug me. For the first time, I am scared of how much more cancer they will find. It is hard to face everything that will come alone, all the healing, and all the bandages. Please. I need a hug."

He stood there; looked at me; and said, "I can't do that." Looking down Tad shook his head.

I was standing in the hotel room, ready for surgery in a short time, wanting a little reassurance that *someone* in the flesh was there for me; and my husband of twenty-seven-plus years has turned and walked away from me when I needed him the most in our entire marriage. Just a hug and a little reassurance were all that I asked for.

The room seemed to be melting all around me. Then, through my sobbing, a light came into my heart and said, "Trust in me. I will never leave you." At this point, the rude awakening came that with the Lord God, I am never alone. With my husband, Tad, I am often alone. I would put my faith in something that I could not see or physically touch because God would always be with me, no matter what happened. God offered me hope. With a smile on my face but sadness in my heart, off I went to begin another surgery, *alone.* Tad was instructed by the nurses to not leave the waiting room at all before, during, or after this surgery.

Jane's surgery was first. She also needed to have her lymph nodes removed due to having more cancer there. She was still asleep when I saw her being wheeled into the recovery room. We have both again written notes on our chests to remind the nurses and doctors who we are. The surgical team has a very good sense of humor, and they were all giggling and whispering as they compared our notes.

The nurse said, "Okay, Thais. Your sister is finished. It is now your turn."

The nurse removed my *good riddance cancer* bracelet and promised to keep it safe.

They were all laughing, and so was I until the mask covered my nose and I was instructed to count backward from a hundred. I remember saying ninety-nine.

What Day Is This?

Thursday, February 6, 2003
very black night, Thursday morning, 2:00 *a.m.*

My *very* noisy roommate is gone; and there is a wonderful, healing silence. I'm not sure where she came from, but she descended on me like a nightmare in the middle of the night. She was old, maybe seventy years or more, and delirious, talking and screaming. I know that the hospital is completely full and overflowing, but I was not resting.

Now, due to this screaming roommate, I have had hours on end to lie awake and think about cancer. Time to wonder, "How does one survive this ordeal?" Repeatedly, I heard in my mind God saying, "I am the light. I am the way."

In those wee morning hours, when it is only me and the quiet, I have much time to think. My closest friend seems to be a flashing green light beeping on a machine with its slow clicks. The machine is letting the air in and out on the leg massager so I won't get a blood clot. It almost sounds like rhythmic breathing—slow, steady, and constant. It seems to be the only thing slow and constant in my life at this time. I still have a lot of healing to do.

I have six inches of tubing for drainage that is surgically implanted in my axillary area under my right arm, where the nodes were. Before chemo, I will have another surgery to place a port in my chest. If the chemo drips out of the port, it could mean plastic surgery to repair the tissue. There can be permanent damage to your heart. There is also the little thing of no hair for months on end.

I now have a swollen, throbbing arm. I will have six months of chemo, with all of those great side effects, and two months of radiation to look forward to; and if I am one of the fortunate ones, I will be alive in five years. I tell you truly as I lay in this hospital bed at 2 a.m. that it does make you think. It takes an inner strength that comes from deep within to fight cancer. We all don't have this ability. Mine comes more each day from the only one true God that is growing inside of my heart—also from the wonderful friends and family that support me. This they do in prayers and thoughts, in ways that they will never know the depth of; and I will never be able to repay. I think more than I need to and too far ahead. It is only time and now I have too much idle time to think.

I must pull from within and realize that my focus is, and should be, on God, for He is the master healer and I am but his servant. I stop to pray and say, "Thank you God for this day and these people that are making me comfortable now." Then my heart is at ease and I know that all is right at this time and I will deal with tomorrow, tomorrow. I will awake joyfully in a few hours, for I will have been given another day on this earth. Only then could I fall into a deep, healing sleep.

It is now late midmorning. I am awakened by an ever-growing cadence of many feet marching together in unison. Is this a dream?

The roaring sound stops; and around the corner of my room, my surgeon, we will call him Dr. Wonderful—sticks his head in the open doorway. "Good morning, Thais. How are you feeling?" He listened to my weak, "Okay." He said, "I have a few students with me. Would it be all right for them to come in and examine you with me presiding?" I said, "Well, of course."

At this point, my body feels as if it weren't my own, so why not share in education? Dr. Wonderful entered into the room with his entourage of young and very attentive students that were hanging on his every word. God had given me the head surgeon of the University of Michigan and a group of awesome students. Could I be in better hands?

Around the corner came my own entire group of students, straight out of any hospital show on television today, in their white coats with clipboards in hand. They were looking very intently for their next cue. Each one had the opportunity to examine a different aspect of my surgery. Talk about the Discovery Channel on your own body. I am learning *so* much.

Now it is time for rest. Dr. Wonderful said, "You can go home a day early if you would like."

In my head I was thinking, "No not really; but I sure didn't get any sleep last night, and I know that they need the bed." What I said was, "Okay, I know that you need the bed and I'm doing alright."

It is a three-hour drive home, so I pray that I don't have a complication anytime soon. The day was sunny, and the roads were clear, so I'll just sleep awhile now and go home a little later. God is so great.

Home Sweet Home

Friday, February 7, 2003
very cold, ten degrees

Frost crystals glisten on the window pane. This is my first day home after my fourth trip to U of M and my third surgery. Tad and Laurelin left early for work and school. It is very cold, and it has snowed about five inches of white, beautiful, fluffy snow. It is the kind of snow that I would have liked to make angels in when I was a child. Today, I could use an entire host of angels. I began to move this morning and realized that my body aches—every muscle and every inch of my body is in great pain. I really couldn't move too much because I felt like someone had parked his dump truck on top of me and left for the evening. Certain movements couldn't be done yet without great pain.

I slowly moved around my own quiet house, put in a load of wash, had a cup of tea, and wrote a letter. It took an incredible amount of time to move any part of my body. I called some friends, and it was so good to hear their voices. I combed my hair that will soon be gone and brushed my teeth. My tongue was numb. It was an odd feeling. I took a shower. The warm water felt so good.

I wanted to see the horses, so I had to dress. I couldn't lift my arm. A loose-fitting button shirt was a good choice. A pair of Tad's sweat pants looked very inviting as I pulled them on.

I then collected my dogs, the cats, and horse treats. We all headed outdoors into the sunshine and freezing temperatures to see the glory of God. We then pushed and shuffled through the snow out to see the horses. It was sunny and *so* cold at 10:30 a.m. The cold penetrated my skin and awakened new senses. What a great day to be alive.

These days, now more than ever, I thank God for each day and every hour. I thank him for letting me feel the pain because feeling it makes me realize that I am *alive*. Khanada and Laddie are very happy to see me, lots of head-bobbing and whinnying. They smell so good. After my soft pats on their warm fur and those gentle knickers from the horses, it is off to the mailbox.

The snow is a perfect white and gently cradled on the tree branches. My movement is extremely slow, and the animals run ahead and come back to wait for me. Each and every step is well-executed and thought-out to produce the least amount of pain.

Next was lunch at home with Laurelin. How I love her. After a good, warm lunch with great conversation, she left to return back to school. It was now a good time to check e-mails. There was a wonderful birthday card from Matt. It brought tears to my eyes. I am the most fortunate mother in the world to have Matt and Laurelin. I love them so.

The pain medications make me tired. I lay down with all of my warm, furry friends for a nap. I fell into a deep, restful, quiet sleep.

Lori, Travis's mom, is a nurse; and after work, she was kind enough to come to the house and help change my surgical dressings. There are many to change. What a good person she is. Tad has been to the chili supper at the school, so he brought home chili and bread for dinner, along with groceries.

He is trying to help in the ways that he wants to help. What I really need from my husband is a big hug much more than groceries and clean dishes. Tad and I sat in the same room and watched the movie *Sweet Home Alabama.* He even stayed awake. I'm so tired, but I wanted to sit by him.

Tad has gone into the other bedroom to sleep now. This is something new.

I can see the moon out my bedroom window. I hear my owl friend calling for me in the night from the forest, saying "Whoo. Whoo. Whoo." Deep is my trust in God. I opened my Bible, and this is what I happened to open to, Psalms.

> But I trust in your unfailing love; my heart rejoices in your salvation. I will sing to the Lord for he has been good to me.
>
> Psalm 13:5–6

I am at peace now. A deep, healing sleep encompassed my tired, painful body.

Not Such a Good Day

Monday, February 10, 2003
7:30 a.m. another gray Michigan day

There is much deep snow on the ground. The snow does help take away the grayness of the sky. At least the ground is white. A light snow is falling now. I enjoy having Laurelin here. She can always help out, even if it is not her favorite thing to do. Matthew is at college more than an hour away with no car to drive from college to home. I prayed today that Matt and Laurelin will have a day that runs smoothly for them.

Laurelin is amazing with the help that she offers to me. I thank God that she is at home. Yesterday was Sunday; and Lori, Travis's mom, could not get here through the snowstorm to help change my bandages. I couldn't do these by myself; and Tad had stated, "I can't help you at all." Thank God that Laurelin was home. She reached for the bandages where I could not and changed them for me. She then rubbed my aching shoulders and put cream on my skin in places that I could not reach. I had asked Tad for help; but he said, "I can't do those nursing things," so instead he did dishes and watched television.

Today, my body hurts and is extremely painful. This is a new feeling of pain. The drain to remove all the extra fluid that my lymph nodes would normally remove is partially plugged. This is not a good thing. I wish that I could be away with no aches or pains, no chemo, no surgery, no ports, and no radiation, with someone who could just hug me. I think that I could take hugs for hours and hours and hours and never grow tired of them.

But it is good to be alive today, and someday I will have all of that. My family and friends have helped me immensely. My tongue is numb. My shoulder is numb, and so is my breast. My underarm and back arm to my elbow has a painful prickling sensation, like when your leg is waking up from being numb.

The hands are both great. What a blessing. Again, God is by my side. I haven't taken any pain medicine today, and feel like an elephant sat on me. But my prayer beeper from the church is going strong, and it makes me smile and takes away some of the pain each time it beeps. Then I know that someone in our church is saying a prayer for me.

Tuesday, February 11, 2003
very windy, snow, blizzard conditions, eighteen degrees

At 8:oo p.m. last night, it started snowing and blowing. You could not see one foot in front of you as the bitter wind blew the snow so violently. It hurt your lungs to breathe in. Comfort outside could not be found.

The horses were in all day, and that rarely happens. Monday night, I hurt so badly under my arm that Lori, Travis's mom, came and helped to change the bandages this morning. We both tried to get the clot that had formed in the tubing to move down into the plastic drain that was inserted into my armpit. The clot would not move and was slowing down the drainage from the site. I was in pain everywhere. At 9:30 p.m., it was getting worse. I decided to walk out to see the horses, and the snow was up to my knees.

Now I was in pain and worried about Laurelin because she wasn't home yet. When Laurelin made it home, I rejoiced. I was so sore and achy and I thought that a warm shower might help with the pain. I noticed drainage on my shirt from the site under my arm. I bent over to remove my clothes and then blood and lymph fluid gushed out of me like a garden hose that had been turned on high.

It was so unbelievably gross! There was deep red blood everywhere. It was on the carpet, sink, and counter. I jumped into the warm shower and started to clean myself up. I thought maybe the warmth of the water would get the clot moving. I got out of the shower and was standing naked as I looked into the mirror and saw the plastic tube for drainage inserted under my arm. This was the drainage tube that was not working as it should. I felt extraordinarily sick to my stomach.

What an incredible mess. I lay down on a large towel on the bed so I wouldn't pass out. I cried and cried and cried. Tad heard me crying and sent Laurelin in to see what the problem was. Laurelin came into the room, and shock registered on her face at what she saw.

She came to my side, held me close, and comforted me. Thank God for my daughter, Laurelin. She let me rest for a while. She then began cleaning up what I had not yet finished. She came back later to help with that miserable drain that was inserted into my skin. She was an immense help physically and emotionally. I felt better. We cleaned up everything, and it was all so repulsive. But what a strong woman God has made in my daughter. She made tea for herself and me while Tad watched TV.

Now, as I write, I am feeling a little better. I am going to bed very soon. God, thank you for my daughter Laurelin. She has set her needs aside and taken the time to show compassion for another person.

First I must finish writing. We have received over twelve inches of snow today alone. I am now lying in bed and can see the large snowflakes gently falling. I realize that God has made each snowflake unique. Not one is the same. We, as humans, are all unique also in our bodies and our experiences. This, I can say, has for sure been one unique experience that I could have skipped. I am not sure how cancer fits into the plan that God has for me. I understand that God, the Great Creator, knows what he is doing. My job is to follow God, have faith, hope, and wait on the Lord.

I can do all things through Christ which strengthens me.
Philippians 4:13

"For I know the plans I have for you," declares the Lord, "plans to prosper you and not to harm you, plans to give you hope and a future. Then you will call upon me and come and pray to me, and I will listen to you. You will seek me and find me when you seek me with all your heart."
Jeremiah 29:11–13

Be joyful in hope, patient in affliction, and faithful in prayer.
Romans 12:12

Hope and prayers are abundant. Now I have to work on the patience.

Another Cup of Kindness

Wednesday, February 12, 2003
sunny at last, cold

Woke up today, and I don't feel as bad as yesterday; but I really feel dragged out. My surgical site is pink. That is usually not a good thing. I'm not excited about that. This morning, I was able to get cleaned up quite well by myself in spite of the pain. I even washed my hair, the hair that will soon be gone, and I took a long hot shower.

I had an appointment with my chemotherapy doctor today, Dr. Kindness. I was so sore and hot, and I felt horrible. Tad did offer to take me to the doctor's office since he didn't think that I looked well enough to drive. Dr Kindness looked at the site of my most recent surgery under my arm. She also could see that I didn't feel well at all. She called my surgeon at the University of Michigan. These two doctors used to work together at the

University of Michigan. How lucky for me. They are both very concerned. They made the decision that I should be hospitalized due to an infection; I needed to spend at least three to four days on IV antibiotics. I knew that I felt like death warmed-over and I would do whatever it took to feel better.

Dr. Kindness gave instructions to Tad to take me to the emergency room at the hospital and said, "Don't leave Thais until she is in a room at the hospital for the night." Dr Kindness called ahead to the hospital to let them know that I was coming. She told the hospital that I should be admitted and what type of treatment that I should receive. It was getting late in the day, and I was feeling very dizzy and much more sick as the minutes passed.

Tad took me to the emergency room, walked in with me, gave my name to the nurse, and sat me down in a seat to wait. He said, "I am leaving to go get Laurelin."

"What? She is seventeen years old, and *I* need *you* now, here in this place with me!"

He walked out and just left me sitting all by myself in the waiting area of the emergency room, sick with infection and almost hallucinating in pain.

Finally, I was taken into a room in the ER; and after four times of trying to get an IV into my arm, it was accomplished. By this time, I was in and out of consciousness and feeling much as I imagined a pincushion would feel. In the ER, they gave me morphine, and I could feel it rush up my arm. It was hot and gave instant relief of some pain. Now I understand what it feels like to get an immediate drug high. I was beginning to comprehend what a drug-induced rush was.

I instantly felt better and wanted to stay in that state. This IV number four had finally worked. When I was transported to another room, the IV was lost out of my arm; yet another nurse had the opportunity to pin the IV on Thais. Again, I was alone for most all of this. Where *was* Tad? He showed up with

Laurelin, and she took over as my family while Tad sat in the other room. Her hands were soft and warm as she held mine.

Finally, I was moved into my own room out of the ER. At this point, again, the IV was compromised, and the nurse had to relocate another site. My arm was sore and black and blue.

Morphine; sleeping pills; pain medications; a warm, soft hand; I don't remember much else. I do remember a nurse that was very kind. She spoke with me, washed me, gave me a massage, and gently moved my aching body. I think she had angel's wings on her back because when she moved, I could hear them flutter.

Thursday, February 13, 2003

More intravenous needles had to be inserted somewhere on my body that will stay and give me more medicine, and again there were more blood draws. My entire hand and arm were extremely sore. Tad and Laurelin came in after Travis's swim meet. I think he swam well. I just remember that I hurt a lot. Lori, Travis's mom, came to visit and brought me a gift; it was an angel of friendship. I need any and every angel that is possible.

Friday, February 14, 2003
sunny, cold

Today, I had many visitors. Hey, I just realized that it is Valentine's Day. I feel a little better. I got cleaned up; Shari and Jeanne came with candy and flowers. Dr. Kindness came and assisted with the bandages. She gave me a positive report. Even though she will administer chemotherapy and many things that in a normal life I would steer clear of, she always fills my cup with kindness. Today, I had more wonderful visitors, and some are cancer survivors: Beth, Jill, Jackie and Deb. Tad's parents, Tad, and Laurelin also came.

Tad gave me a leather case for my passport with a promise that as soon as I feel better, we would go away together, just the two of us, on a trip to an island. This was something that we had never done, but I had always wished we could do together, just the two of us. We are always saving for a trip in the future that never comes. Again Tad has promised a trip for just the two of us; but this time I believed I saw a tear on Tad's cheek. Could this be a new beginning for us? I love them all so much, and they all care a great amount for me. God, I realize that you have given me these friends and family members to make my life richer. Thank you.

Saturday, February 15, 2003

I will get to go home soon. I am feeling better, but really I do not have much energy. I have gotten all cleaned up in anticipation for going home today. Last night, my IV came out *again;* and I lost hours worth of medicine. The nurse was so frustrated. She was frustrated? I am beyond that! In her frustration, not realizing what she was doing late at night in a darkened room, the nurse placed the IV outside of the vein, into the tissue. The medication and the fluid were trapped in between the layers of tissue instead of circulating throughout my entire body. For the last two hours, I had been watching my arm grow larger with all of the fluid that cannot be reabsorbed by my body. I had repeatedly called for the nurse. The pain was again severely great.

I just won another day in the hospital.

Monday, February 17, 2003

I am home now and I have severe vertigo. I can't even stand up straight, and I am by myself at home after a doctor's appointment. When I stand, I have such dizziness that I need to hold the wall or something stable so as not to fall over. The room is spinning whether I am standing, sitting, or lying. My stomach feels sick. I feel as though I am in constant movement.

Tad did drive me to the appointment with my chemo doctor this morning. No way could I have driven. Dr. Kindness said I would start chemo on February 26. I can't wait. I have to start these toxic chemo drugs to get finished with treatment for this cancer. Today, I can't even stand up without falling over.

Today I took another trip to the local surgeon to have him diagnose if it was time to remove the drain. He said that it should come out, and my mind started to wonder. "*How* it would be removed?" This thing is six inches long outside of my body, and six inches are inserted inside my body and stitched into me. *How* would he remove it?

Clip, clip of the stitches; and he pulled it out of me in one swift yank. That hurt, but it actually feels better with the thing gone. What a day.

Thursday, February 20, 2003

Rest; rest; and again, more rest. I have no idea what day it is, only that there is constant movement in my head. My existence has been reduced to dizziness, movement, pills and more of the same. Friends have come to visit and they needed to assist me out of bed to a chair to visit for a short while. They helped with everything that I can no longer do for myself. Then later during the day another friend came to help me with standing, sitting and walking. I am reminded by each of my friends that my condition is temporary and that they *want* to help me. This has actually come as such a comfort because I cannot count on my stability when I try to stand and Tad and Laurelin are gone during the day. It is so odd receiving so much help; I am usually the one helping. I guess that God thought I could be humbled a small amount and receive from others.

Saturday, February 22, 2003
cold and sunny

I have to get out of the house. I am the type of person that would rather stand in a snowstorm than be cooped up in the house for days on end. Tad can sense that I need to have a diversion; I think that he needs one also. We drove to the casino in Michigan City and played for hours on a small amount of money and we won a small amount. I was sore. My vertigo is better but I needed support from Tad's arm as we walked. It was nice that he offered his arm with no discussion; it made me feel warm on the inside to be close to him. It was a good distraction for both of us from what has become our daily life.

Sunday, February 23, 2003
glorious sunshine, cold, twenty two degrees

Even though I am very sore, it has been wonderful to go to church today and see people at the service. They all have such kind words of support for me. In the axillary region under my arm and also by my breast, it feels so different—numb, tight, stretched.

Monday, February 24, 2003

Today, I went back to work from my week's vacation in the hospital. It went well. I need to work. I can't risk losing my horses. If I don't make my regular pay, Tad will want to sell them. They aren't worth anything to anyone else and are much less a month than the country club and the golfing trips that Tad plans so frequently for the spring with his friends. Those horses are getting me through some very difficult times now. I can't lose them.

Tuesday, February 25, 2003
cold winter day, snow, twenty one degrees

I worked again, and I still need to send out notes to people. When I got home, I was very tired and sat down in a comfy chair for a short while. I woke up in the morning, still sitting in the chair. Had Tad not seen me asleep there?

Wednesday, February 26, 2003
cold, dark, more snow, twenty three degrees

Today is my first day beginning six months of chemotherapy. I am tired, and I need to take the drug Antivert for vertigo. I can barely stand up straight or walk without looking like a drunken sailor. I have shopped for groceries, and there are many healthy foods in the refrigerator. My friend had brought me to my appointment and stayed as long as she could. Tad met me at chemo after my treatment was finished to bring me home.

They won't let me drive home by myself. After chemo, I had many great calls from friends and families. I can't wait to feel normal again, although I don't think that it will be any-time soon. I have not had any nausea. I do have written directions of when to take the vast number of pills that were given to me. I think these tablets are keeping the sick feeling away for now. Thank you, God, for bringing me through this day.

Thursday, February 27, 2003
dim, cloudy, cold, sinister feeling day

Today, I am experiencing a bit of brain fog, but no sickness. The day seemed to be moving in slow motion. Thank goodness that I had changed my work days so I could be off today and not miss any time off from work. I had to get a shot to prevent infection and increase the blood counts. What will they think of next?

Saturday, March 1, 2003

Tired. I am still exhausted. I am still working full-time, going to chemo appointments, and trying to take care of a huge home. I am trying to manage all of these things while I try to rest and heal. I just realized that Mom and Dad will be coming home soon from Florida. They will need help when they arrive back home.

Sunday, March 2, 2003
radiant sunshine, forty two degrees

Today I felt that I had to get out of the house and have a change of scenery. I asked Tad to come to the Meijer Gardens with me to see the hatching butterflies. He said, "I have to go to work and catch up." He is working Sundays now? I went to the home show in Grand Rapids and went to Meijer Gardens to see the butterflies. They are so stunning. They make me think of the rebirth that my body is going through now. The butterflies were so beautiful, colorful, and delicate when they first hatched. They sat and gently moved their wings for hours to dry them out and see what they felt like when they accomplished movement. This is something new and foreign to them. It is a new hope in a new body. Will I ever feel that way? I felt that I had to try getting out of the house for something other than work, but I am so extremely tired.

Monday, March 3, 2003

I worked today and again I am extremely tired. So what is new? This is much harder on my body than I had ever imagined, but I am *alive*.

Tuesday, March 4, 2003
sunny, bright blue skies

Today, I had an appointment with the skin doctor to remove some areas that appear suspicious, hopefully not cancer. The nurse at the skin doctor appointment said, "Good luck with all of your treatments for cancer." She also said, "I can't wait to see you when you are healthier." At that moment, I realized that I was a cancer patient undergoing chemo therapy, not someone else, *me!* Boy, I want to live; but I am *so* tired. I will try some vitamins and acupuncture and see if it helps.

> Do you not know? Have you not heard? The Lord is the everlasting God, the Creator of the ends of the earth. He will not grow tired or weary, and his understanding no one can fathom. He gives strength to the weary and increases the power of the weak. Even youths grow tired and weary, and men stumble and fall; but those who hope in the Lord will renew their strength. They will soar on wings like eagles; they will run and not grow weary, they will walk and not be faint.
>
> Isaiah 40: 28–31

Wednesday, March 5, 2003

When I arrived home tonight from work at 6:00 p.m., I was *so* tired. My back was terribly painful. I thought that a soak in my large tub would feel good. I fell asleep in my big, warm bath. I woke up hours later in a cold tub. Is there anything normal left in my life?

Thursday, March 6, 2003
damp, cold, light fog rising on the remaining snow

I was very tired when I woke up in the morning. How is it possible that I could be tired after sleeping in the warm water in the bathtub for hours and then finishing ten more hours of sleep in bed?

I spent the morning on the phone trying to straighten out the charges for the treatment that I am receiving. I had an eye doctor's appointment today and then lunch with, Jeanne. Lunch with Jeanne was absolutely great.

This afternoon was my first appointment with Jamie. I had seen an article about her in the newspaper before I had cancer and had saved it for months, thinking that I would call her for an appointment. She is a nutritionist and a master herbalist. What a great combination. I had talked with her and found out that she had an opening to see me today.

I got very lost in Grand Rapids. I don't travel there often. I was confused about the directions and upset because I was almost late. I knew that I was close to her address, but close doesn't count when you have to be on time.

I saw a man exit an art gallery and stopped to ask him for possible clarification of the directions. I asked him if he knew of the address. He stated that he wasn't familiar with it. He asked what the person's name was. I said, "Jamie." He looked at me and said, with a welcoming smile, "She is an awesome massage therapist!" His name was Rene, and Jamie was a personal friend. He couldn't say enough nice things about this woman that I was about to see. He gave me directions and two copies of his new CD, one for myself and one for Jamie. Not only did God help me select a person who has a personal association with her, but also I met an artist who performs vibrant Latin music.

It amazes me how God keeps giving, even in small ways. It makes my relationship with him stronger each day.

The strange thing after taking time for my conversation with Rene is that I met Jamie exactly on time. She was very tall, with dark hair flowing to her waist and a smile that just pulled you in. She was for me a fountain of knowledge, a complete encyclopedia in the human form—a registered dietitian, a massage therapist, and beautiful at that.

I feel much more at peace with the decision to do chemotherapy because with her guidance, I will have the least amount of destruction to healthy tissues as possible. She suggested that I get back on my blue green algae and other antioxidant products. She was very happy that I had been eating organic for years and supported staying on this program. The one thing that she did point out was that stress can cause many types of illness. Reduction of any stress would always be a good health move and exercise was very important.

Friday, March 7, 2003
sunny and cold

I had to work at 7:00 a.m., so I really didn't sleep well, thinking that I might miss hearing the alarm and oversleep. I worked 7:00 a.m. to 1:00 p.m. It was a good day, and I am back on my natural vitamins. I am not so tired today. I took my first walk in months. I shared some of my great week with Tad. After hearing all of the incredibly wonderful things that had happened to me this last week, he seemed very concerned that I didn't have only *one* doctor, instead I had numerous specialist doctors. He seemed much more concerned about that than what condition my health or state of mind was in.

I've asked Tad so many times for a back rub. My spine has been painful for over a week. When I ask him to please rub my aching back, he says, "I can't do that." This is the same man that has joyfully made children with me and I have shared my most intimate thoughts and feelings with. We know each other as no one else will ever know us, and he can't rub my aching back? I will have to set up a massage with Jamie even though it will cost money, which will not make Tad happy. I hurt so incredibly bad.

How Did I Get Here?

Saturday, March 8, 2003
*gloomy winter day, gray, dismal, hanging
clouds, dirty snow, no sunshine*

Last night, Friday, Tad had chosen a movie and we watched it
together. It was very depressing but had a good message. The
father left his son at a very young, impressionable age. The son
became a drug user, killed someone, and had a son. The father
then took his son to jail after they reconciled. I have enough
drama in my life. I needed a happy movie.

My friends are having a big party tonight, and Tad said
he couldn't go to the party unless it was before 7:00 p.m. He
knows that I want to go, and he knows that it starts at 7:00
p.m. What else is he doing on a Saturday night?

Sunday, March 9, 2003

Last night, I went into the bathroom to brush my teeth. Tad was in the other room, reading the newspaper. I looked into the mirror and wondered; *how did my life get like this?*

Here I am with a husband that can provide everything *but* love, especially when I need it the most. He worries about money when we have it and when we don't.

I had gone to the party with my friends last night because Tad was not available. He was with the guys, doing whatever they wanted. I needed a diversion from this life I'm leading. No. I needed a diversion from this life that is leading me. When I was at the party with my friends I laughed, cried, and danced. I shared with others about my children at the exhilarating party. The music was loud and fantastic, the conversation great and the food was fabulous. I forgot for a short while that I had cancer.

Last night, after the party, Tad came home shortly after me. I asked, "Where have you been? It is very late."

He said, "I have been at a card game." I asked, "Where were all of the wives on a Saturday night?" "Out," was all he said. He turned and walked off into the guest room to sleep.

I went to take a long, hot shower. I removed my clothes and wig. I stood looking at my naked body in the mirror. In the mirror, a *stranger* appeared to be staring back at me. There, I stood looking into the eyes of a woman that had completed three surgeries for breast cancer. Her hair was falling out and would be gone within days. This woman had many scars, and I saw the pain she carried throughout her entire body. This woman is living in a huge house with no one who could just hold her, touch her, or love her. Then I realized that it was *me* in the mirror, not the stranger that it appeared to be. It was *me.*

How did I get here?

Had I taken the wrong turn in life somewhere? But which turn, when, where?

I cried, totally out of control for thirty to sixty minutes, great, huge sobs and irrepressible screams of total anguish. The tears flowed like torrents and waves of raging water. I screamed and screamed still louder at the top of my lungs. I thought that if I could scream loud enough maybe I could make the hurt inside my heart and outside of my body completely go away.

It was late into the night, and Tad never came to see what was happening with me. Somewhere in the wee morning hours, I finally fell to sleep with my animals all cuddling very close to my body. They were trying to comfort me in those dark hours. I realized that I was truly all alone, void of human companionship when I needed it most.

My sleep became deep and constant. In a dream, or maybe it would be called a vision, God came to my side. He stood close, looking at me, with gentle and penetrating eyes then said, "Read Psalms 121. Read this scripture that I have made for you."

In the morning, when I awoke, I read Psalm 121. These are extremely powerful words.

> I lift up my eyes to the hills—where does my help come from? My help comes from the Lord, the maker of heaven and earth. He will not let your foot slip—he who watches over you will not slumber; indeed, he who watches over Israel will neither slumber nor sleep. The Lord watches over you—the Lord is your shade at your right hand; the sun will not harm you by day, nor the moon by night. The Lord will keep you from all harm—he will watch over your life; the Lord will watch over your coming and going both now and forevermore.
>
> Psalm 121

The pain of the surgeries is still the same; but the pain in my heart is much less, for I know that even in the darkest hours, God will be with me, he offers me hope. I know that unless this ache in my heart goes away, I will never fully heal inside or out. Excellent diet, chemotherapy, surgery, and radiation will surely help to cure the cancer but won't cure a broken heart. Only God has that power. I want to just be a whole person again. I am nothing that my husband needs or wants anymore, and I haven't even lost all of my hair yet. I am now just a thorn in his side.

> The righteous cry out and the Lord hears them; he delivers them from all of their troubles. The Lord is close to the brokenhearted and saves those who are crushed in spirit.
>
> Psalm 34:17–18

> He heals the brokenhearted and binds up their wounds. He determines the number of the stars and calls them each by name. Great is our Lord and mighty in power; his understanding has no limit. The Lord sustains the humble but casts the wicked to the ground.
>
> Psalm 147:3–6

> His pleasure is not in the strength of the horse, nor his delight in the legs of man; the Lord delights in those who fear him, who put their hope in his unfailing love.
>
> Psalm 147:10–11

It is Sunday now as I write about last night. Matt called tonight. He and his girlfriend made it back from Colorado in a horrendous snowstorm, home to Ohio. They sound very happy. They had a wonderful vacation. He is so concerned about me and said, "Should I come home?" My answer, with a great sadness in my heart, was, "No, Matt. I am fine." Fine? What is the definition of *fine? Fine,* as referenced in the dictionary would be *very well*—not me. *Thin,* as in "thin hair" could be me. *Unpleasant* as in "extremely unsuitable or undesirable"—that could be me. I need to choose my words better.

Who Is Baking the Bread?

Monday, March 10, 2003
cold, wet, gloomy

This morning I noticed a soft lump under my right breast where the lumpectomy was performed. Could this be another infection? It feels hot, and this is about where my infection was less than a month ago.

At night, I sleep with ice packs on the incision areas. These areas are very painful. I believe that the additional pain is from the infection that I had. The skin feels taut and tender, and the stitches are still healing. If the ice pack melts, I go to the freezer and search for the frozen bag of peas. It really seems to give me much relief to have the cold resting on the incision area. If all else fails, they can be consumed for meals.

Massage is a great relief also, but of course I have to pay for that. Tad does not like the additional costs because insurance doesn't pay for this service. Jamie has been so kind to hardly charge me anything.

Last night, at about 3:00 a.m., I ran out of ice packs and packages of frozen vegetables. The twenty ounce size of frozen vegetables fits perfectly, but there were none left in the freezer. I had used them all. The family size is much too large, and I can't control the area it is to stay on as well.

At 3:00 a.m., I was in great pain and needing a frozen pack. After exploring in the freezer on a rampage of pain and anguish, I found the perfect shape. The problem was that it wasn't pliable; it couldn't be shaped. I took some more pain medicine, went back to bed, and gently placed the plastic bag of frozen bread dough on the incisions with a thin towel by my skin so as not to get frost bite. I am a smart woman but, at this point, a desperate one. I fell into a deep sleep.

I had the most wonderful dreams. I was whole again, with no cancer; and I had plenty of beautiful auburn hair. The children were small, and we were together in the kitchen. Matt and Laurelin were baking with me as we had always done when they were small children. They often got more flour outside the bread bowl than inside, but we shared so much fun and laughter. What an awesome dream of a very joyful time in our lives.

When I awoke, I thought that someone was playing a trick on me because I woke up to the smell of fresh-baked bread. Not believing my nose, I opened my eyes; and under my arm, the complete loaf of bread had risen and was encompassing my entire arm and chest. This was the largest loaf of risen bread that I had ever seen and smelled, and it was attached to me.

I looked to the heavens and laughed and laughed. My God certainly has a sense of humor.

Tuesday, March 11, 2003
cold, sunny, bright

My hair is coarse and brittle. It is starting to fall out. I see more hair on my bed pillow every day. When I wash my hair, I hold it in place so as not to disturb it or make it come out any faster.

When I was in Florida with my sister, I had purchased a human hair wig to wear when my hair fell out. This wig I had purchased looked exactly like my hair. We even asked the opinions of other costumers in the store. They had no clue that the wig wasn't my own hair. There was a very fun wig that was long, seductive, and strawberry blonde. The tresses of hair flowed long and lovely. I had almost purchased it; but at the last minute, at the cash counter, I returned it to its original resting place among the other locks of love. I chose the natural-looking, shorter style and the mid-length sassy, auburn bouncy hair. This bouncy auburn wig would be my *fun* hair. Maybe losing my hair would be acceptable because now I had two wigs—one natural and one for fun.

Wednesday, March 12, 2003

This is a bad hair day. I had to pull all my hair back into a clip so it wouldn't be falling into my patient's mouths. By the end of the day, the weight of the clip pulled much of my hair out of my scalp. I repositioned the clip numerous times during the day, and I had to use copious amounts of hairspray. Fortunately, I made it through the day with hair still attached to my head. This is *not* a good thing. I was warned about losing my hair and how soon it would happen, but when, which day?

Thursday, March 13, 2003
cold, wet, dreary, thirty two degrees

I went to see the physician's assistant at the chemo office today. I'm worried about this lump in my armpit. Today, I am wearing about half a bottle of hairspray to hold my own hair on to my head temporarily. I went home after my appointment, knowing that the doctor was not sure if there was a new infection at the incision site.

I went into the shower to wash out all of the hairspray. With the force of the spray of the water in the shower, I could hear the hair pulling out of my head. I could physically hear each end of my hair ripping out of my head. I decided to use the shampoo and see what would happen. As I washed with the suds, there were hunks and masses of hair in my hands. It looked like I was holding a wig, and the horrific part was that it was *my hair*. I jumped out of the shower.

I was trying to keep my cool as I spoke out loud to God. He reminded me, "I will never leave you. Hair or not, you are my child." I dried my hair with the towel, and much more came out. At last, I tried the hairdryer; and it just blew my hair out of my head in masses. Nothing was going to keep it in now. When I finished the shower ordeal, I looked into the mirror. I was a middle-age woman with scars on her breast, complete bald spots on her head, and some patches of hair on the scalp still clinging to her head. At this point, I may have been *slightly* vocal; and Laurelin rushed in and stared at this new person that had overtaken her mother's body. We looked at each other, embraced each other, and began to cry together. We both said, "Good thing Travis is a swimmer." Those swimmers know how to shave heads, and soon he will shave it off.

The next part of my day took me off to the vet's with the dogs and the new wig. I figured that wearing my wig to the vets would be the trial run to see if anyone noticed that this was a wig. The new wig felt so strange. No one could tell until I pulled it up to show them.

My acupuncture appointment was next, with a new doctor that I didn't know. Maybe I shouldn't have pulled off my wig at that appointment, because she spoke no English and became slightly scared of me. Oops. I had to adjust my wig often. This could become a bad habit.

At my acupuncture appointment, the pain areas showed that my intestines, tongue, and liver are under stress. I guess that should be of no surprise since I am on chemotherapy, and how about the rest of me? Do I think the rest of my body is under any stress? How could *that* be possible? Stress, surely not!

Friday, March 14, 2003

I am tired and hurt so much. I am excited that I will get to see Jamie for a back rub. The one and a half hour massage was fantastic. Hopefully it will move the chemo out of my body. She thinks that I have another infection. I do also think that something is very wrong with me. I don't physically feel well. Mentally I am dealing with major hair fallout.

I do feel so much better after seeing Jamie.

Home at night, on my knees again in prayer, I ask, "God, can you heal the pain in Tad's heart? God, can you give me the strength to do whatever your will is?"

Outside of my window, I see the large owl in the tree and he says, "Whoooo."

Saturday, March 15, 2003
sunny, brisk day, thirty seven degrees

Today is the hay auction sale. I need hay for my horses to eat. Tad never helps with this. I am always on my own because these are my horses, not his. The bales can sometimes weigh as much as eighty pounds, which is usually not an issue; but I had surgery less than six weeks ago and was hospitalized three weeks ago for an additional infection. But my horses must eat, and again I am on my own.

God has a plan for me and has brought more great people across my path. The men at the hay auction helped load the hay that I had bought today. Tad was busy. Even though he loaded trucks for years, loading is no longer his kind of job, nothing to do with injury. Everyone asked where Tad was, and of course, as usual, I made excuses. These men even came home with me to unload the hay bales because they knew that I just had surgery recently and they wanted to help. Am I not the most fortunate woman on earth, to have such compassionate friends?

God, you are so kind to put these men in my life when I really need them. Later, I came out to ride Khanada. What a wonderful ride. It feels so good to move with such large strides and big, effortless movement. I completely feel free of *everything*.

Sunday, March 16, 2003
warm, sixty five degrees

It is Travis's birthday today. Today is very warm for Michigan at this time of the year. Matt and his girlfriend had come home from school for a Sunday dinner. Sunday dinners together are one thing that our family has always done. This is a wonderful time to catch up on what has happened in the previous week and make sure everyone is ready to tackle another week. Today, before dinner, Tad and I went for a walk in Saugatuck at the state park. The trail is in the woods, and hiking to the beach on late winter trails at this time of year can be very slippery. There was much ice and snow, with steep drop-offs. I walked where it was safe today, on the prairie flatlands; and

Tad walked where he wanted to, not with the dogs and I. So much for Tad and I doing something together.

I had a wonderful dinner with all of the children and Tad. It was an Irish dinner, celebrating a birthday and our family heritage. It was so good to see the kids. The evening was warm. Matt and his girlfriend left to return to college.

Travis, with clippers in hand, then took me outside and sat me down in a chair on our covered, wraparound porch with very little excitement. I had been wearing the wig for a few days because my own hair or lack thereof, was falling out in large sections and was extremely ugly. I had felt that I was test driving the wig. I was getting used to it and how people responded to me wearing a wig. Their response was none. People had no idea that my hair had been falling out for days and that under my wig, very little was left. I was trying to get comfortable wearing it before all of my hair was gone.

I was now sitting in the chair on the porch of my house; much like Matt had done when I trimmed his hair as a child. Travis flipped on the switch and started the clippers. About ten seconds later, what was left on the porch was a large pile of *my* hair.

I looked into the window to use it as a mirror. I stared, and the first words out of my mouth were, "I look like G.I. Jane." I touched my head; and it was prickly, like the rough side of Velcro. I looked like I had joined the army. I was looking into the window at an image of myself with no hair at all. Travis said, "Don't worry. It grows back." For him, this was a yearly occurrence with much pomp and circumstance for swimming. But I was a forty-eight-year-old woman, wife, and a mother who could barely swim, who had *not* joined the army, and who now didn't have a stitch of hair on her head. I looked into the mirror and realized that God had given me a nicely shaped head. "Thank you, God." I realized then that my nicely shaped, bald head was *cold*.

Monday, March 17, 2003

I worked. I ate. I slept. I pulled on and adjusted my wig. I seem to constantly tug and pull it down when no one was looking.

Wednesday, March 19, 2003

Today, the war broke out in Iraq. It greatly saddens my heart to see our country entering a war. It is one small world. I am trying to stay alive, and men in different countries are ready to kill each other. God, please explain this to me.

Chemotherapy

Thursday, March 20, 2003

I felt good as I awoke today. This is yet another chemo day. Tad is too busy at work to take me to chemo and pick me up. Laurelin is at school, and I can't drive myself home. Jeanne offered to take me and stay as long as I needed her. I dressed for my day and placed on my *good riddance cancer* bracelet that I wear to every appointment.

My chemo lasts about six hours. First, they have to find a vein. Next, they start some medication to be sure that all is good with the IV. I have the choice of sitting in a recliner or lying on a bed. I usually choose the recliner because I always fight so to not go to sleep. Why? Does anyone really care if I am asleep or awake? It has been hard to get a vein, but Melissa is my nurse. I believe that she is a gift straight from God. She can get the IV inserted correctly the first time, every time. A warm pack first, and then a few taps on the vein, a small bit of conversation and hocus pocus, and the needle is in with no pain. I pray each night, that God keep her in his hands and continue to let her use the talent that God has given to her. She always has a kind word and a big smile.

As the chemo medicine started to run up my arm, I could feel heat running through my veins. It made my entire body warm, and I became half awake, half asleep. My eyes became very heavy and my body very relaxed. My mind wandered to when the children were small and I would take them down by myself to our beach. There, we would spend hours playing in the sand and surf, making sand castles. I would envision how wonderful our time in the future as a family together would be. Sometimes, when you get to the future, what the reality actually is seems more like a nightmare. I have to realize that this nightmare too shall pass.

With chemo medicine running through my veins, I dreamed of white, puffy clouds. I was in heaven, dancing on beautiful white fluffy clouds. My heart was so joyous. There were many other people, or were they angels? After all, I was in heaven. I couldn't really tell who they were, nor do I really need to know or care to know. We were all singing and dancing. I could hear the tambourines, cymbals, lyre, and harp. I know that God was in our presence and he was taking great care of his children. My heart was so full of love. We were all praising Him. "How great thou art." This was absolutely the best party that I had *ever* been to.

> The trumpeters and singers joined in unison, as with one voice, to give praise and thanks to the Lord. Accompanied by trumpets, cymbals and other instruments, they raised their voices in praise to the Lord and sang: "He is good; his love endures forever."
>
> Chronicles 2:5–13

My heart is steadfast, O God, my heart is steadfast; I will sing and make music. Awake my soul! Awake harp and lyre! I will awaken the dawn. I will praise you O Lord, among the nations; I will sing of you among the peoples. For great is your love, reaching to the heavens; your faithfulness reaches to the skies. Be exalted, o God, above the heavens; let your glory be over all the earth.

Psalm 57:7–11

I heard someone calling my name from a distance. It was someone calling me to leave the party to go home. It was Melissa waking me after six hours of the chemo drugs dripping into my veins to wipe out any possible cancer.

I am amazed how God takes care of me. Here, he has given me a glimpse of what heaven would possibly be like. Now I will go to my home to eat and sleep. My friend Jeanne was there and had been sitting on guard with me the entire time, reading a book. She has been my earthly angel, watching over me to be sure that I don't fall from the chair, that an IV doesn't become loose or any other reactions that could happen during chemotherapy. I truly have a host of angels to take care of me.

Friday, March 21, 2003
warm day, fifty five degrees

My heart still feels joyful, but my body needs rest and many pills so that I don't get sick from the chemo. Melissa has written down when I am supposed to take each of the pills.

Today, I went for a ride on Kahanada. She's always so dependable. For such a large animal, she is extremely gentle. Being with Khanada brings my body and soul such a great peace and respite from the pain.

Monday, March 24, 2003

When I was at work, I had noticed a red area on my skin about two days ago.

It seems to be getting worse, so I went to see my chemo-therapy doctor today at lunch. She thinks that it might be a follicular dermatitis. Something else new, it always seems to be something.

Tuesday, March 25

More of the same skin sores. These seem to be mostly on my midsection. I am beginning to understand what a leper in bib-lical times may have felt like and been going through.

Wednesday, March 26, 2003

More skin lesions. Obviously, this medicine is not working; they are on my trunk, lymph nodes area, back, and other areas, following in a line. Could this be shingles? What else could happen? Maybe I shouldn't even ask. On my agenda for the day was an appointment with the chemo nurse and doctor. They both confirm that I have shingles. Shingles! I thought that only sick people got them. Oh wait. I have cancer; scars; a reduced immune system; no hair; and dry mouth, nose, ears, and throat. My new best friend is a pharmacist, and I have a direct line to the pharmacy. They know me by name. I guess that one of the above could put me into the sick category.

Wait, I should be looking on the glass as half full, I am alive to experience all of these wonders that a body can go through and still be here to write about it. I am not sure if it is more emotionally or physically exhausting, or probably it is a combination of both. I'm dealing with a husband that has checked out of our relationship and a father that is trying desperately to find movement and a life after a severe stroke. I am working my full time schedule, progressing through cancer treatment, caring for our family and home; and God each day you bring me through it all! My dear Lord you are wondrous! Our days are so limited on this earth. In truth, I feel that I could have used many days more wisely. The reality at forty-eight years is; there are some good days, some bad, but many may have been wasted.

I want to dance in the moonlight and walk on the beach, laugh with my children, and go to Europe. I want to ride my horses and be with a man that can still love me even though the outside may look different. My friend always says that if you are still alive God isn't finished working in your life. This I need to remember. I always figured that if I ever needed anyone for love and support my husband, the love of my life, would always be there for me. Oh wait. That is emotional stuff, and he's not good at that. Whatever happened to better or worse? My spouse is good for making a house payment and doing dishes—all important things, but anybody can do them. The emotional stuff may make him dig deeper than he cares to go. My outward changes will be temporary. I am still the same person on the inside, screaming to be set free.

The night is quiet. Pollix, my beautiful Nova Scotia Duck Toller is one of my best friends. He and my collie, Pumpkin, are the most loving dogs. They are getting older and falling apart like me. They are constant companions and always by my side, loving me unconditionally every minute of every day. The three of us are falling apart together. I love them so.

They are my comfort now in the night when I sleep alone in my bed—a bed that has never had just one person sleeping in it. This is the bed that I so enjoyed loving my husband in, cuddling close and laying in each other's arms, talking, kissing, and lost in love. It is now a very big, lonely bed. Tad sleeps alone upstairs in his new bed and seems so distant.

These Shingles can be extremely painful but I don't hurt too much. "Thank you, God, for this day."

Is this Spring Break?

Thursday, April 3, 2003
clouds, gloom and plenty of rain, thirty eight degrees

Brrrr! The weather is typical Michigan weather. Isn't this what makes the grass and flowers grow? This is my spring vacation, the first day of ten days of unpaid vacation. Tad said he would take off a day or two this week.

This morning, I took Khanada out for exercise on a long lunge line for twenty minutes. I cleaned out drawers and paid bills. How can I stand so much excitement on vacation? When I was in the hospital, Tad had promised me a vacation just the two of us, alone, together. Is this what he meant about taking me on vacation with a passport? Today's prediction is for more rain and more cold. It hardly feels like a tropical island vacation alone with my husband.

Today, I have an appointment with a master herbalist; and she will help more with diet and herbs to return me to health.

I am to keep up with eating more grains, and she has given me some new herbs to take. I also have acupuncture. I think that the acupuncturist only speaks Chinese because I can't understand a word she says, but she smiles, and I feel better.

Tonight I am in bed by 9:00 p.m. This is early for me.

Friday, April 4, 2003
cold rain, dark ominous skies, thirty three degrees

It's the second day of vacation, and Tad has chosen to work every day that I am home. So much for any vacation together *anywhere*. This day is full of cold air. It has turned out to be another gray day with guess what—more cold rain.

I wanted to be by the horses and hear their knickers, so I groomed the horses in the barn in the morning. I love it when no other people are there. It is like having your own place. What shiny coats my horses have under all the dirt and excess hair of the winter. I brushed away the dirt and grime from their winter coats. I wish that it was as easy to brush away the grime of life.

Laurelin went to exercise in the morning; I'm not quite up to that yet. She came home for lunch, and we had an enjoyable conversation about Travis and the upcoming formal event. Laurelin and I researched restaurants in Chicago to dine at before their formal dance. This is a yearly dance and dinner for the Hope College swim team and their dates. They usually go to a location away from Holland, and the big city is always wonderful. We found the perfect restaurant in Chicago, called them, and made the reservation for eight people. I am sure that they will have a wonderful time with their friends. I drove to the bank made deposits and home again. There are always more bills to pay, and it is bill pay day. Didn't I *just* do this?

I took the dogs out for a walk to the barn to check on the horses. The horses smell so good. They whinny at the sight of me. I love these noises that they make. This is such a peaceful, quiet place. All of the animals' eyes are bright and shining. They are all looking at me with gentle eyes and greet me with unconditional love.

Walking home from the barn, I observe shimmering, icy branches, and the thirty degree temperature penetrates my bones. There was a fine mist of rain. The ice on the trees looked like diamonds. The tree branches were glistening all the colors of the rainbow—indigo, violet, magenta, and fuchsia. The rain continued to come down as a fine mist. Everything looked like an ice castle shimmering, and it was very slippery. It appeared to be raining but froze as it hit anything. This weather can be beautiful but very deadly.

Laurelin and Travis are going to Chicago. I pray that it warms up by tomorrow. Matt is with his girlfriend in Ohio visiting her parents. Boy, they sure are in a different place than where I am. They are certainly having more fun. I pray, "Dear God, please protect and comfort my children."

I touched my head because it was cold, and I realized that it is still noisy when I run my hand over it. I will never think of Velcro again in the same way. Sometimes, I forget that I have no hair. Sometimes, I even forget that I have cancer; that is God giving me a short reprieve from my life. I really feel so physically all alone, almost like I am on an island—married but without a husband. He seems to worry about everything good and bad except not one concerned look cast in my direction—not a smile, a hug, or one touch for me.

Wednesday, April 9, 2003
cold, wet, thirty seven degrees

I have been on spring break for eight days, so I decided to work a chemo appointment in on the ninth since I wasn't going anywhere. My friend Maggie came with me since she was on break and Tad wouldn't take a half hour off work to drop me off for a chemotherapy appointment. He basically takes off any time of the day that he wants to for golf, meetings, lunches, and vacation. But it seems that I am not as important as a golf date with friends.

When I got to chemo, Melissa, the best nurse ever to get an IV started, is not there. Another nurse is taking her place. Melissa is on vacation, and we should all have vacation. Wait I again realized that *I am* on vacation. Is that what you call this cold, wet week, a vacation? What happened to the idea of an island vacation?

After the third time of trying to get the IV started, I was getting a little sick. I don't think that this nurse has had much experience with getting an IV started—ever. Maggie decided that she would take over this horror film and cast a new nurse. The next nurse was great. Thank you, God that Maggie was there to take control. She read magazines and a book while I was in la-la land. What a great chauffer. She took me home, gave me dinner, and got me into bed.

After chemo, for a day or two, I can't think straight, curved, or backward; everything seems to go in slow motion—thinking, speech, and movements.

Blessed is he who has regard for the weak; The LORD delivers him in times of trouble.

The LORD will protect and preserve his life; he will bless him in the land and not surrender him to the desires of his foes. The LORD will sustain him on his sickbed and restore him from his bed of illness.

Psalm 41: 1–3

Life and Living

Friday, April 11, 2003
sunny, sixty degrees

Off to Jamie's in Grand Rapids for a massage from 9:30 to
11:00. I think that Jamie has angel wings. I think that they are
tucked under her shirt. Her friend, Rene, that I met the first
day that I was looking for her has sent to me, through Jamie,
a CD of music he has made. He is extremely talented and a
very handsome, young Latino man. He has very dark hair and
those beautiful, piercing, dark brown eyes. I am truly a sucker
for brown eyes.

Jamie had a gift for me, and I had made her some jewelry.
She has suggested green tea. I will get some. I feel so good
after seeing Jamie. My body feels light and no longer in pain
for awhile. My heart soars when I see her.

Going home, I stopped for shopping at Hobby Lobby, went to get groceries, and then head home. This afternoon, I had enough energy to clean the wood floors, vacuum, dust, and clean the glass table tops. This is the most energy that I have had since the last surgery. Between the chemo and working, it is taking all the energy that I have to get through a week.

I went out for a ride on Khanada. Of course, Laddie wants attention also, and I am running out of steam. I attached the lunge line to him and let him canter around me for twenty minutes. He finally stopped and came in for treats and hugs. What a horse!

The day was warm and bright—about sixty degrees—and I needed a light jacket. The sky was a deep blue in color, and the breeze was lightly touching my skin. This day, the weather was so much better than the thirty-eight degrees of a few days ago. The grass is beginning to sprout, and all of the animals are very happy. This was a spring day that God had made. The best part is that I am alive here on God's earth to see and feel the goodness that he has given us on this day.

I realize that Laurelin and Travis are a huge help in taking care of the house. Matt is away at school and does what he can when he is home. I have no cleaning lady and am trying to work my full schedule, help Mom and Dad, go through surgeries for cancer, have chemotherapy, and run a household. Along with all of that, I have the emotional uncertainties of the fact that when I really need my husband the most in my entire life, he is not here for me.

When you have a five-bedroom home, there is always much work to be done. Matt and his girlfriend are coming home tomorrow for the day so we can have a family dinner. I love it when my whole family is at the table together with great conversation.

Tonight, I took a quick shower. Wow. I realized again that my hair is gone. Zip. Zero. Completely gone. I started to wash my hair, raising my hands up to grab it and wash the shampoo through it, lifting from behind; but there was nothing there. It is just gone. Will I ever get used to that? Now I had to rinse and rinse all the shampoo off. If I get used to not using shampoo, I may be able to save a dollar and put it toward that trip Tad promised to the island. Okay. Next was the dry down. I can rub and rub it like I have seen the servicemen do. The men in the Middle East now fighting for us have no hair, and they are men that are extremely brave. That is what I need to be now: very brave.

> Do not be anxious about anything, but in everything, by prayer and petition with thanksgiving present your requests to God. And the peace of God which transcends all understanding will guard your hearts and your minds in Jesus Christ.
>
> Philippians 4:6–7

Thoughts Late at Night

Friday, April 11, 2003

It is late at night. I can't sleep. My mind is racing. Is it the chemotherapy or the steroids that I now get with each treatment to quell the pain that is building in my joints? I always thought that when we moved to this little town our family would find God together and become a closer family, with God at the head of our family. In this town there is a church on every corner. The first question asked of me always was, what church do you go to? So church and God must be part of the threads that bind the community together. They must have good high standard of morals, correct?

For years, I have wondered what happened or didn't happen. Could all of this *past* have begun to place a wedge between Tad and me? Could all of this *past* have anything to do with having cancer now?

I came with Tad, who was starting his dream job, and our two children to start a new life together as a family. Tad and our entire family would live in a small old rental in the new area together until our *other* home on Lake Michigan sold. All indications were that our home would sell fast because it was a gorgeous, wood, contemporary home that we had put hours of blood, sweat, and tears into. After thirteen years of marriage, working many jobs and renting homes, this was the first home that we purchased and we had built it together.

The backyard we named deer forest because there were many tall, stately trees; acres of underbrush; and a bountiful number of deer. Our windows at the house on the first floor were about six feet tall, standing only six inches off the floor. Some of the walls were entirely windows. Many times, at dusk, the children and I would lay on the floor in the living room, and deer would come up to the windows and stand and look at us as they ate whatever was outside the windows. They were extremely tame. At times, when walking in deer forest, we would come upon a deer; and we could get almost close enough to pet it. It was like living in a fairy tale. It was always mystical and magical, not ordinary in any form.

It is so difficult now to hold back these thoughts, I must write.

In our front entryway, I had found and purchased the most beautiful hanging lights. When the morning sun shone through the cut, beveled glass, there were hundreds of rainbows on the walls of our home. It was like God's artwork from common, ordinary things. Our mantle above the fireplace was a beam from a local barn that was more than a hundred years old.

We had lovingly chosen each of the trees and bushes in our yard. We had placed them exactly where we as a family envisioned them, bringing splendor in their ripe, old age to our family home. The walk to the beach was short, and this was something we did together often as a family. On a windy and wavy day, we could sit outside and hear the turbulence and fury of the lake; and thank God we lived no closer than we did. Matt was five and Laurelin was three years old when we moved in. We had stained and finished all the woodwork inside and out, just to save a penny.

This was the home that our children would grow up in. Our dream was that someday, our grandchildren would come to visit Tad and me in this home as the years passed and our hair grew gray together. We actually lived there maybe two years.

Racing Reflections

It is three in the morning and my mind won't stop until I write it all down.

Our new rental home of eight hundred square feet was a complete contrast to our home on the Lake. It was small, had carpets that smelled of smoke and pets, was in the city and was extremely affordable. We paid nothing to live there. It belonged to the schools where Tad worked and it was scheduled to be torn down. We chose to live there because we could keep our family together and not have an additional payment.

We had no stove, no refrigerator, no shower, and no washer or dryer for almost two years. I cooked *everything* in an electric wok—breakfast, lunch, and dinner. To save money, we nearly always ate at home. We, on a rare occasion, would go out to a restaurant and eat; but not often. I purchased ice daily for a cooler, which now had become our refrigerator since we had none. This was to be only temporary until our home sold. Our home had been situated on four acres within walking distance to Lake Michigan. Living there the short time that we had was slow and easy like living at a beach house. It was unique and priced to sell. The surprise was on us. Shortly after placing our two thousand plus, square foot home on the market and moving the bare essentials into our new rental, the Middle East invasion happened. Homes in the area stopped selling.

We would sweep into our home on the lake for weekends with a mountain of laundry to clean, this to save money at the Laundromat. After that we could rest and relax. Then we would pack again for the hour plus drive back to our rental to reorganize our lives for the next week. Of course, weekends were when the people wanting to purchase a home on Lake Michigan wished to view our home. This made for some interesting weekends.

We lived about six months like this and I began to wonder if it was a dream. No. Actually, I began to wonder if it was a nightmare. I could see that temporary was much longer than I had imagined. I spoke with Tad about, "Please could we just purchase a used stove and refrigerator for the rental?" I was often answered with, "No it is temporary."

Our rental was for sure a unique home with its own unique experiences. As the wind blew that winter, the glass rattled and the snow accumulated in a drift on our bedroom floor. I never complained. On some mornings, I laughed at the fact that when I woke up in the morning, I could make snowballs without leaving my bedroom. Matt and Laurelin thought this was great fun.

In the spring, we had a robin that liked our home so well she made a nest between the windows. We saw her build the nest with each tiny stick, piece of grass, and bit of yarn that she could find. We could check on the progress of the babies daily and watch the mother while she fed them. It was a wonderful distraction from our life on a daily basis.

This life went on for more than one and a half years. My electric wok was tired. My body was tired. Tad was unhappy most of the time and always stressing about money, even though we had no payment in the rental home. There was nothing "normal" about our lives. Something just wasn't right.

We finally had a "solid" buy sell agreement on our lake home. These people were excellent prospects and had already been approved for the loan, closing was in two weeks. We no longer had the desire to build another home we just wanted a "real" home. We found one and placed a bid. We closed on that home the day before we closed on the lake home. We now had a house that we could make *our* home.

God had yet another plan. No, we didn't close on the lake home because at the last minute, the new owners couldn't get financing. So here we were with a much larger problem: two homes—two homes with two home payments.

At this point, some of us in our family turned toward God and some turned their backs on him, maybe thinking that relying on something that you can't see or hear would not be strong and relying on a person would be better. Tad began to show that relying on himself might be the best answer. After all, isn't it the movers and the shakers in the world who get things done? We now had everything and no foundation to a relationship. Together, in our relationship, we had nothing larger than the both of us that we could count on in a difficult time. We had everything: the job, the house, and the children—everything except God as the center of our relationship.

Somehow, through all of the cancer and chaos here, I found God as the center of my life. These are really true feelings of knowing God intimately. As I face cancer, surgeries, chemotherapy, and radiation, I know now more each day that I need God in my life as my leader. He will always be there for me and will never fail me. Things can be difficult and tough, but he will always walk with me. I will need God to help me bear the pain and uncertainties of life.

Now I will pray to God that he helps me to get through these chemo treatments. I feel that God is working through Jamie using her soft voice, knowledge, heart, and hands to heal me.

At forty-eight years of age and being married over twenty-seven years, I never dreamed of sleeping without my husband night after night. I feel a total separation from the main body as though I have been set afloat in a raft to survive by myself. I feel the loss of the possibilities of dreams together that may have come. I am sure this would not be one of them. This is a nightmare. Without my partner next to me I love to feel the warmth of the dogs and cats. I can hear them breathing the breath of life and I adore them for always being here and not leaving me alone.

I have raced through the finish line with all of these thoughts. My body and mind are tired. My eyes are heavy and my heart is exhausted. Now I shall sleep deep and long.

I sought the Lord, and he answered me; he delivered me from all my fears.

Psalm 34:4

The righteous cry out, and the Lord hears them; he delivers them from all their troubles. The Lord is close to the brokenhearted and saves those that are crushed in spirit. A righteous man may have troubles, but the Lord delivers him from them all; he protects all of his bones, not one of them will be broken.

Psalm 34:17–20

They will no longer be plundered by the nations, nor will wild animals devour them. They will live in safety, and no one will make them afraid.

Ezekiel 34:28

Cancer Days

Sunday, April 13, 2003

I am thankful for my children, Matt, Laurelin, and those who love them. I thank God for my mother, father, brothers, and sisters, their families, friends and my patients. I am grateful for God, sunshine, blue skies, buds on the trees, and the grass that is so green. I'm thankful that I've known Tad during my life. I cherish animals large and small and how they love each day no matter what, so unconditionally.

I am so grateful for Jane. We truly are becoming more like sisters each day. She lives in Toledo and is about four hours away. We talk on the phone and e-mail each other very often. We've laughed, cried, and shared our fears, our dreams, our days of treatments, and our lives.

After our last surgery, Jane started radiation and I started chemotherapy. In a few months, she will be on chemotherapy and I will be on radiation. Our clinical study and surgical treatments mirrored each other but, at this time, are in the reverse order. We can contribute to one another's knowledge of what each of us are experiencing at this stage of treatment. She is not working now; she is taking off during treatment. Ted is back on the Great Lakes, sailing. Her two boys are about the same ages as Matt and Laurelin. Jane is also going through the search for colleges with their youngest son. Her oldest boy is finishing up the year away at college in the same time frame as Matthew.

On one such conversation, we laughed when I said, "Now we both look like G.I. Jane!"

My hair fell out first, but after a while, we both had heads as smooth as a baby's bottom. It seems that when one of us is down, the other is able to build that sister back up again. Too bad you can't hug through the phone. We shared treatments; infections; ideas for comfort; and above all, we had shared a clinical study. We both had a very positive outcome in the study, and we shared the power of antibodies.

It is so odd how many similar things we share. Is it not strange that such a wonderful friendship as this could come from something as scary and debilitating as cancer?

Monday, April 14, 2003
it's a balmy seventy five degrees

Cancer isn't fun. These could very well be some of the hardest, longest, happiest, and emotionally draining days of my life. Extremely hard because you can get over one bump in the road to then hit another when you are not prepared. The longest thing is the waiting: waiting for test results to come, hair to grow, or the chemo to drip through your veins. The happiest thing is you are still alive. You can smell the newly mown grass, kiss the ones you love, and see your children grow older each day. It is emotionally draining because you keep it up day after day after day. Cancer doesn't care if you are rich, poor, short or tall, fat or thin. You could be the president of the United States or the homeless; it just doesn't discriminate.

My tongue, throat, and the inside of my mouth are incredibly sore. The tissue is raw, red, and sloughing. It is extremely painful. My throat is so dry I can't sleep. I have night sweats and hot flashes. My chemotherapy IV arm is sore and needs ice. My ankles are swollen. My feet hurt, and my ear aches—but I am alive.

Today, I laughed and cried in the same sentence. Tonight, I cried and cried and cried by myself. There is no one here to hug me or give any comfort late at night. My cancer didn't go away, and I didn't feel any better after crying and crying.

Completely numb, I walked out onto our covered, wrap-around porch. With my body and mind deadened and null of feeling, I sat on the porch and stared into the black night. In the western sky, I could see dark thunder clouds rolling across the fields toward my home. The temperature dropped and the wind became violent as I stepped onto our grass lawn into the now lightly-falling rain. The turbulence was electrifying. Then fierce pellets of rain were brutally hitting my body, and the wind violently tugged at my clothing as the lightening was brilliant off in the near distance. I realized that I *could* still feel something. With my arms raised to the heavens, I shouted to God, "I want to feel again! I want to live! I want to feel love deep in my heart again. Let these torrents of rain beat on my body so that I can be alive and feel again. Wash over me and cleanse me!" I stood there for what felt like an eternity. Goose bumps covered my entire body. I was cold, wet, and alive. I walked up the stairs to the door, opened it, and entered. My body was filled with energy, I couldn't sleep. I was exhausted and wide awake as I fell into my bed, alone again.

Now, as I write, I think about my friend that was forty-six years old who had a heart attack yesterday. She is lying in a hospital bed, and the doctors are trying to figure out her new plan for life. She is a co-worker, a dental hygienist like me. Last week, her plan seemed fine. On Friday she worked, picked up kids, and danced at night in a show. On Saturday, she had dinner out with her husband. On Sunday, she forgot to pencil in a heart attack. It happened anyway. She is younger than I am and dances tap at least two times a week. How could this happen? She is so young and healthy.

I feel like I need a break from all this, to burst through all of the pain. Maybe I need a little garden and some great weather; a time to just *be,* a time to just be with God in nature, to listen to the birds, the crickets, and the frogs; a time to lie on freshly mown grass with the sunshine on my face and look for hours at the clouds rolling by. Those days have always been days that filled my soul with happiness. On those days I could lie on my back in the newly mown grass, feeling each blade in between my fingers, and just looked into the sky for hours, finding in those white puffy clouds a turtle, dolphin, or dragon. The imagination is the limit. I would roll over, face the grass, and breathe in deeply the smell of Mother Earth. Opening my eyes, I would look for four-leaf clovers. Yes, this is time to just *be.* Dear God, I am asking for a time to just *be.* I am also putting in a request for a new body, that would also be awesome.

But now I have to pray for my friend that is lying in a hospital, recovering from a heart attack. I pray for her and all the others who need my prayers tonight. I thank God again for such a great day to be alive, to be able to feel the pain that I have. I just now rolled over in bed and smelled the freshly picked daffodils that were in my garden today. They are on my night stand next to my bed, bringing joy to my soul. I enjoy their bright, happy color like the sunshine. It was eighty degrees today and will be thirty-nine degrees tomorrow. Welcome to Michigan in the spring.

The Lord is my light and my salvation—whom shall I fear?
The Lord is the stronghold of my life—of whom shall I be
afraid?

Psalm 27:1

Teach me your way O Lord; lead me in a straight path
because of my oppressors.

Psalm 27:11

I am still confident of this: I will see the goodness of the
Lord in the land of the living. Wait for the Lord; be strong
and take heart and wait for the Lord.

Psalm 27:13–14

Therefore, since we have been justified through faith, we
have peace through God our Lord Jesus Christ, through
whom we have gained access by faith into his grace in
which we now stand. And we rejoice in the hope of the
glory of God. Not only so, but we also rejoice in our suffer-
ings, because we know that suffering produces perseverance;
perseverance, character; and character, hope. And hope does
not disappoint us, because God has poured out his love into
our hearts by the Holy Spirit, whom he has given us.

You see, at just the right time, when we were still powerless,
Christ died for the ungodly. Very rarely will anyone die for a
righteous man, though for a good man someone might possibly dare to die. But God demonstrates his own love for us
in this: While we were yet sinners, Christ died for us.

Romans 5:1–8

Friday, April 18, 2003

As a survivor, you need the will to live, but life will get very
tough. A person needs the will to live longer and know that
someday, it will be better. I know now, as my faith in God
increases each day, even though I cannot see it, that my life

will get better. I know this just as I know that there is one God. Even though I can't see him or hear him, I do believe.

Jesus replied, "I tell you the truth, if you have faith and do not doubt, not only can you do what was done to the fig tree but also you can say to this mountain, Go, throw yourself into the sea, and it will be done. If you believe, you will receive whatever you ask for in prayer."

Matthew 21:21

Consider it pure joy, my brothers, whenever you face trials of many kinds, because you know that the testing of your faith develops perseverance. Perseverance must finish its work so that you may be mature and complete, not lacking in anything. If any of you lacks wisdom, he should ask God, who gives generously to all without finding fault, and it will be given to him. But when he asks, he must believe and not doubt, because he who doubts is like a wave of the sea, blown and tossed by the wind. That man should not think he will receive anything from the Lord; he is a double-minded man unstable in all that he does.

James 1:2–8

Blessed is the man who perseveres under trial, because when he has stood the test, he will receive the crown of life that God has promised to those who love him.

James 1:12

Wednesday, April 23, 2003
sunny, fifty seven degrees

Today, I was called in to work, another hygienist was sick. I had a headache for most of the day. No. It was not a headache; it was a migraine. Not much fun. I went for a blood draw at my lunchtime. My white count is down today. If it gets too low, that is not a good thing; and I may have to miss a chemotherapy appointment or change drugs. My cancer is best killed with the regiment that I now am on. I want to finish this treatment that will save my life.

Yesterday, I received another very nice card from a patient and dear friend. I also saw another patient who has health problems. Her husband is a kind and loving man. He has a spinal cord injury, and she has a neurological disease. They are both kind, compassionate people. I must remember to keep them in my prayers daily. Today, I spoke with a friend whose wife recently has passed away from cancer. I will keep him in my prayers.

They are all so concerned for me. How could this be that they care so much? I am only an ordinary person, but my friends and family say that I am trying to live an extraordinary life of love and compassion. Oh, God, I need more guidance each day. If I show others something that is above ordinary, it is to the glory of God, not to the glory of me.

Today, the yellow and purple violets are awakening. They opened and yawned to a bright blue sky and a temperature of about fifty-seven degrees. Oh, what a day that the Lord God has made for me.

Thursday, April 24, 2003
sunny, sixty degrees

I worked again. It is amazing that I feel well enough to work five straight days in a row. My white count is very low: 1.9. Any lower, and I will need to change my treatment. Today, God has given me the strength to keep going. *Please, dear God, I don't want to be sick anymore.*

Matt called from college, and he needs to be out of his college apartment tomorrow, not in three days like he had thought. Yikes! Matt needs help, and Tad isn't available again; he will be out golfing with friends. Well, I work from 7:00 a.m.

to 1:30 p.m., and then I guess that I can drive the one and a half hours to college to help unload the apartment. If I needed Matt's help, he would be here for me.

Friday, April 25, 2003
white, puffy clouds in the sky softly floating, sixty two degrees

Dad always said, "When you see white, puffy clouds, good things are coming your way." Let's hope that he is right. The grape hyacinths opened today with their heady perfume. These are Matthew's favorite flowers, and today he is coming home from college. What a welcome it will be! God, you are so good to your children.

This will be a marathon day, hopefully filled with Samson's strength. I woke up at 5:30 a.m. and was off to early work. I got out of work by 1:30, rested one hour and drove to Kalamazoo to help Matt. God, I am grateful for children, grateful for the deviation they give me from my cancer life. I am grateful for their smiles and warm hugs and their constant energy and love that they pour out to me daily.

I have worked all day, and I am exceedingly tired. I arrived at Matt's apartment in Kalamazoo at about 5:00 p.m. Again, although we need Tad's help, he is not here. Matt and I packed and cleaned. We moved so much stuff from that college apartment. We finished about 10:30 p.m. Is Tad still golfing? He seems to always be busy when he is needed and available when you really aren't desperate for his help. The apartment looked great. Matt is sure to get back the large security deposit. Next, it was the one-and-a-half-hour drive home.

Then there was the small chore of unpacking the entire car. Tad was sleeping and would not get up to help. Finally, after unloading the entire car that we had loaded only hours earlier, Matt and I went to bed by 1:00 a.m. It is so nice to have Matt home again. As a mother, you want them to grow and begin a life of their own; but it is always so nice to have them under your roof for conversation and support.

I do not have the strength of Samson. Before I closed my weary eyes, I opened my Bible to read:

> Do you not know? Have you not heard? The Lord is the everlasting God, The Creator of the ends of the earth. He will not grow tired or weary, and his understanding no one can fathom. He gives strength to the weary, and increases the power of the weak. Even youths grow tired and weary, and young men stumble and fall; but those who hope in the Lord will renew their strength. They will soar on wings like eagles; they will run and not grow weary. They will walk and not be faint.
>
> Isaiah 40:28–31

Saturday, April 26, 2003
cool in the morning, forty two degrees,
and a balmy sixty three in the afternoon

Tad and I went for a bike ride to Grand Haven, about a fifty-mile ride. The air was cool, but the sun was wonderful. I shouted at the top of my lungs with hands thrown to the heavens while riding, "It feels good to be alive with the sun on my face and the wind caressing my skin!" I am grateful for spring. It has been a long winter. The steroids that I receive now to lessen the joint pain of the chemotherapy enable me to do many physical things at times, such as ride that far. I find it amazing that I have the stamina to do this. When I got home, I took a long nap. At least I am functioning as "normal" as possible. Steroids also make me hungry, and I sleep more restlessly. My pain in the joints is more bearable. It's incredibly odd that I seem to be destroying my body to stay alive.

God has given me the will to live, and that is what I want to do. I have researched for hours and hours the possible treatments. I have talked with educated doctors and patients that have been through many different types of procedures. I have tried massage, supplements, diet, acupuncture, surgeries, and chemotherapy; and next will be radiation. I have undergone clinical studies to be alive. Today, I will rejoice that I am alive.

I paid Tad today all of the money that I owe for horses and for my monthly bills he has assigned to me. He is still not happy.

Sunday, April 27, 2003

Today there is no church service. There is an assembly at Van Andale and about twelve thousand people are attending. That is too many people in one place for me.

Today, I realized that most of my eyelashes are gone. I did put mascara on the remaining two eyelashes. Mascara on two eyelashes—am I crazy? Maybe. Laurelin learned in science class that it takes a long time to grow eyelashes back. So what else is new? The steroids are helping with the pain, but there is that weight gain thing. I don't think that bike riding daily will take away the shape that my body seems to be morphing into.

Tonight, we had dinner with all of our family together. I take as much pleasure in preparing a large, full, home-cooked meal as the children and their friends take in devouring it. I do so enjoy the lively conversation between my two children and their newfound friends. I love to hear about college life and to be included in their lives. Tad is home to sit at the head of the table. Today I am joyful.

Living Life with Cancer

Tuesday, April 29, 2003
sunny, cool wind, and sixty five degrees

It happened yesterday.

My friend Mary has helped me through cancer and its daily devastation with her awesome attitude. She had cancer shortly before I was diagnosed. She has been constantly making me feel like the beautiful woman that God wants me to be through the joy in her heart and natural makeup. Today, she has lost her life to cancer. I know that for her, this is a promotion to live in eternity with God. She will be greatly missed by me and by so many of her friends, family, and clients. She was always smiling, with a positive attitude and a good word for us all. What a true friend that God has made cross my path in life.

You see that a person is justified by what he does and not
by faith alone.

James 2:24

My friend is for sure justified in heaven with God. She
was a great woman, kind and gentle. She will be missed on
this earth.

Wednesday, April 30, 2003
morning rain, raging wind, and dark clouds, fifty five degrees

Today, I had an appointment with my chemotherapy doctor,
Dr Kindness. She is compassionate and upbeat. She is like
my very own cheerleader and coach. Dr. Kindness is always
right in there with me every step of the way, with encourag-
ing words and suggestions of how to make the treatment work
better with my body, always educating and explaining each
step as we grow closer to the end of treatment. It went okay.
Back to work tomorrow.

Thursday, May 1, 2003
warm sunshine on my face, the wind has stilled

It is May Day. I went to the barn at 7:20 a.m.; and JC, one of the
boarder's horses, was loose. He had gotten caught in the shav-
ings bin. This was not pretty. He was caught from the front legs
forward into a bin about four feet off the ground. He had nothing to push off from in the front to get back onto the ground.
He was frantic and exhausted from trying to free himself. I
talked with him and tried to make him calm while I dismantled
the fence of boards that he was caught on. Loose, scared, and
now free, he whinnied and took off only to come back to me.
This was the first hour of my day. I gave him an apple and put
him back into his turnout. He bobbed his head, whinnied, and
took off, so happy that he was in his normal place.

I have gotten to know the entire group of horses well. This boarding barn is situated behind my house, it belongs to my neighbors. The boarding fee is reasonable and I help out when I can. I love that it is close and I can walk out to the barn whenever I choose to.

Today, again, I have chemotherapy with my very favorite nurse. I never thought that I would look forward to chemo, but the angel of nurses is back. My hand is still sore from my last treatment because the IV had to be put into my hand. I am running out of veins to put the chemo into. The medicine is destroying my veins and yet making me stay alive. My veins are becoming small, and they roll away when someone tries to use them. That is a difficult concept to get my mind around. Thank God Jeanne, my confidante throughout this journey, came with me. What a great help. I slept and can't remember most of this treatment. Jeanne said I was carrying on a conversation at times with her. I don't remember.

Today is the day that Mary is being buried. I don't even remember most of the day after chemo. This is such a sad day. I am alive, and she is not.

Matt came home tonight to bring me May flowers. To me, this is always the first day of the new season of new life. He never forgets that I love this day. Since he was a baby and he could walk, he has brought me May flowers. I remember him as two-year-old, picking daffodils from our yard, which had thousands of daffodils. He chose each one as if *that one* was a special gift. I see him in my mind, plucking each and smelling it as he put them into his basket. This I definitely do remember.

Tonight after a day of chemotherapy I was in the kitchen with Matt and Laurelin talking and laughing as they prepared an evening meal for us all. I stood up and caught my *good riddance to cancer* bracelet on the edge of the counter, with a loud snap the bracelet shattered. Beads and charms of love went hurling into the air and came down seeking each an individual spot to hide in the kitchen in any nook or cranny that was available. That bracelet had been for me as my *good riddance to cancer,* good luck charm and now it lay on the kitchen floor in hundreds of pieces. I stopped looked at Matt and Laurelin; my eyes began to gush with tears. They both quickly began to scramble looking for all of the individual pieces. Laurelin looked at me and said, "Look it will be put back together like you are being put back together!" Somehow I was comforted by her words and the fact that we had found all of the beads. Jackie could string it back together for me. My bracelet would be all in one piece again just as I had hoped the treatments would do for my body.

Friday, May 2, 2003
sunshine, glorious sunshine

I have an appointment with Jamie today. I wish that I could see her every day. Today, she let me exchange bracelets for an hour massage. My body and my soul feel more alive. Tad and I spoke three words to each other the whole day. "Good day?" "Yeah." This has become our conversation. I want to talk with him about our life together and our children and our dreams like in the old days. Conversation is not on Tad's agenda today.

I am tired, so I turn in at 8:00 p.m. I am so tired of being treated as if I am nothing to my husband, and tired of always having to deal with cancer and the aftermath. I went to sleep and had a dream that God was holding my hand. Can I stay there, holding his hand, forever? He actually says, "No. You need to go back to my earth." To be in such a sweet place was like being on vacation. *Hang in there, Thais.*

Saturday, May 3, 2003
sunny and cool, blue skies, sixty two degrees

It is prom day for Laurelin and Travis. This, of course, is a big day. They are so in love. I can see that they are kind to each other. This makes my heart soar to the heavens. I have such great joy in my children and watching their lives unfold. Laurelin looks beautiful. Wearing a coral dress, with her vibrant, strawberry-colored hair and thin figure, she looks like a vision standing in the sun, having pictures taken. Tad is the beaming father. Travis looks so handsome in his tuxedo with his broad shoulders and big smile.

Matt is home from college and is going out with friends. They are going to the Tulip Time festivities for the "eats" and visiting with friends at home from college. This is a *big* festival day in Holland. I am so proud of both of my children.

How did I get so old to not be going out with my husband and friends for laughter and smiles? How has my life become as if I am walking on eggshells around Tad—no fun, no laughter, no touch, no life together? It has not always been like this. It is cancer, not a death sentence. I realize this, and I am going to live while I am alive here on this earth that God has given to me. I am going to laugh out loud, enjoy friends, dig in the dirt, marvel at God's creations, try something new, eat chocolate, burn the pretty candles, walk in the rain, splash in a mud puddle, stay up late talking with my lover, dig my toes into warm sand, travel, love my family, sing off key, ride bare back and breathe in life around me.

The trillium, my favorite flower, is beginning to open. There are hundreds upon hundreds of them in my woods. The trees are also showing signs of new life. I am beginning to show signs of new life. I think that my hair is beginning to grow.

Saturday, May 24, 2003

Matt has been sick. I took him to the doctors. I think that he is feeling better now. I can't have my children sick. When they are unhappy or ill, my heart breaks. This may be part of being a mother; but we have a very close bond, my children and me. If anything was to happen to them, it would be catastrophic in my life. They are my strength and compassion, my rock and my joy. God says:

> As a mother comforts her child so I will comfort you.
>
> Isaiah 6:1

And again, "I will put my trust in him. And again he says, "Here am I and the children God has given me."

> Hebrews 2:13

Everyone that believes that Jesus is the Christ is born of God, and everyone who loves the father loves his child as well.

> 1 John 5:1

How great is the love the Father has lavished on us, that we should be called children of God.

> 1 John 3:1

Tuesday, May 27, 2003

today is gloomy and dark with a constant drizzle of rain

I went to chemo yesterday. The day was a beautiful day, one made in heaven. I spent it with a chemotherapy IV stuck in my arm. For hours, I was in a state of semi-consciousness. It was as if I was in a fog, in another world that is of this world. Today, my joints hurt badly and I have a cold, which, when you feel like yuck anyhow, is so much more awful.

Today, I saw Jamie, and I gave her the bracelets that I had made for her. Making them for her had been a great escape from my normal world. She enjoyed them so much. She is always upbeat and kind to me.

My joints are unbelievably painful today and I can barely walk. I am now on antibiotics. It has turned out I don't have a cold; it is pneumonia. No wonder that I feel so bad. I am not sleeping well, I am worried, worried, worried about my children's health, Tad, college and bills. I am even worried if I will be alive to worry. It brings to mind this passage in Matthew in the Bible:

> Therefore I tell you do not worry about your life, what you eat or drink; or about your body, what you will wear. Is not life more important than food, and the body more important than clothes?" Look at the birds of the air; they do not sow or reap or store away in barns, and yet your heavenly father feeds them. Are you not much more valuable than they? Who of you by worrying can add a single hour to his life?
>
> Matthew 7:25–27

> So do not worry, saying, "What shall we eat?" or "What shall we drink?" or "What shall we wear?" For the pagans run after all these things, and your heavenly Father knows that you need them. But seek first his kingdom and his righteousness, and all these things will be given to you as well. Therefore do not worry about tomorrow, for tomorrow will worry about itself. Each day has trouble enough of its own.
>
> Matthew 7:31–34

Sunday, June 1, 2003
ominous dark clouds hang overhead, damp, no rain, fifty degrees

As I write, my body is tremendously sore; and there is such cruddy weather today—just gray cold. And I am so sore I can't even ride. I feel extremely old! There is no one at home in these walls to hug me or hold me.

I pray that someday, our whole family will be happy and healthy—all on the same day. Now today, Laurelin came to me and told me that she has a lump in her breast. I began to wonder if I had entered the Twilight Zone. When she said, "I have a lump in my breast," my body sensed a numbness, as if I could melt into the floorboards. The lump was exactly in the same place that my cancer had been taken from me. I would take this fear from her in one second, and if it is cancer, I would take that.

God, she is only eighteen years old and has watched me lose my hair and have surgery after surgery, and she has watched needle after needle being put into me to keep me alive. Please take this concern from her. Dear God, I need help. Please give her and me peace and help me to relax. Please tell me it will be okay. My insides were churning with complete horror and panic! But on the outside I was calm and cool. I hugged Laurelin and said, "It is so good that you told me this. I will call the doctor in the morning and will find out what we need to do. You are so young and I love you greatly."

I will call the doctor first thing in the morning.

I told Tad what was happening with Laurelin. Tears came into his eyes and he hugged me.

The Lord is my shepherd I shall lack nothing.

Psalm 23:1

May the Lord answer when you are in distress; may the name Of the God of Jacob protect you.

Psalm 20:1

May he give you the desire of your heart and make all your plans succeed.

Psalm 20:4

Sunday, June 8, 2003
the sun shows its face, finally, in the evening

Matt seems so happy these days with his girlfriend and so much more healthy. It seems wonderful to see them both laughing and smiling. Tad hugged me again. Other than last week, it has been truly months since he has been this close to me. He feels warm.

I shuffle in great pain, like a person who is old and has lived her entire life and is at the end of her days. My joints are in such extremely intense pain. Many people don't have this pain. God, I always seem to get into the problem line. How did I get into the wrong line again? Please keep hold of my hand tightly. I cannot bear all of the pain and uncertainty of the future without your grasp on my hand and my heart.

I shuffled to the barn, with knees that were on fire, to see Laddie and Khanada. I needed to brush them and talk with them and have their large, warm bodies wrapped around this old, aching one that I now have no control over but live in day to day. These horses know that I am sick, and they wrap their large bodies around me and nuzzled in with tender whinnies. I am now okay and have the knowledge that I can make it another day. I will be better someday. I shuffled home.

When I got home, Tad looked at me and said, "I am sorry that you are in such great pain and so sick." Yes, I am sorry also. He said, "Don't worry about the money for our household needs or the money for college. It will work out. Please just get better." What a load off of me. Was this for real? I fell into a deep sleep like that of a baby. I awoke to a Monday full of sunshine. I realized that my prayers had been temporarily answered and my pain had decreased.

Graduation and Families

It has been so long since I have written, and it is hard to see without glasses. The chemo has changed my eyesight for the worse. Laurelin had her graduation party. Before the party after work each night, I made all of the food for over a hundred people for her party that week. I thought that I could also clean our huge home, but I was exhausted after working three days and preparing food for one hundred guests.

I came into the house worn out from working all day. There, standing, smiling at me, with very large grins, were Travis and Laurelin, dripping from head to toe in sweat. They had taken off the entire day of work to stay home and clean the complete house from top to bottom. The windows were washed, baseboards cleaned, wood floors waxed, cupboards all washed down and sparkling. I just started to cry. There was *no way* that I could have worked my dental hygiene job, made all of the food for over a hundred people, and cleaned the entire home by myself. Did I think that I was Superwoman? I think that even through all the sweat and tears, I distinctly heard the trumpets of angels.

Now it was time for me to rest. Matt cleaned his room and the computer room. Without the three of them, I couldn't have done that party. Thank God for children. The party was wonderful—so much laughter and happiness. I do so enjoy laughter and happiness; can I stay in this place? I must rest now.

The day of the graduation ceremony was rainy. This meant that the ceremony was held indoors, in the great heat and cramped seating arrangements in the gymnasium. It was wonderful to see my youngest child graduate. Six months ago, I didn't know if I would be alive for this occasion.

The overnight party for the seniors was fantastic. I usually always try to help for anything at school, and this was no exception. I wanted to stay up all night with the kids at the bowling and dance center where the overnight was planned. There were card games all night, bowling, a hypnotist, food, more food, and plenty of games to last a night. I wanted to stay the entire night but was just too tired. Tired, I am beginning to see this is a regular routine. I do something, and then I am exhausted. I do something again and I'm still exhausted *but alive. Thank you, God. I am still alive.*

Wednesday, June 11, 2003

Laurelin had her ultrasound a few days ago for the lump; and today, the office called.

They believe that it is non-cancerous; but without a biopsy, the doctors cannot be sure. Since I had cancer, they recommend that a biopsy in the hospital be done. The tumor should be removed.

I'm feeling pretty sick to my stomach about this whole thing and *so* sick of the word *cancer*. I keep hearing from doctors, "Because of your mother's situation ... Because of your mother's cancer ..." I am sick of hearing that. I would take this from her and endure it all again if it would make this go away for her.

I hear my inner voice say, "Thais, rejoice in the fact that they think that it may not be cancer and that a routine biopsy will confirm this." Please, dear God, let Laurelin heal. Let me heal and be free of this terrible word *cancer*. Dear God, I am exhausted now and need to sleep. Please, God, bless my family with happiness and health. Dear God, thank you for my family. Now I must rest.

Friday, June 20, 2003
warm, cool breeze, sun, blue skies; and wispy, white clouds that look like cotton candy, eighty degrees

God, I thank you for all the days that you have given me. These days are icing on the cake. Matt is healthy, eating better, feeling better, and working. He works a strange shift of four ten-hour days, in at 4:00 p.m. and out at 2:00 a.m. I guess it is a shift that a college kid could love. He makes mirrors for cars, and he enjoys it. He says that the people are very good to him and it makes him realize that he doesn't want to do this for a lifetime. College looks better all the time.

Laurelin is working at the local grocery store and doing odd jobs, such as painting and gardening for a family in town. Tad is exercising a lot these days and has become a bicycle maniac, or so he says. He goes often by himself for hours on end. We never know when he will come home. Many weekends, when our family would go to the cottage on the lake for the weekend, at the last minute, he chooses to stay at home.

He says, "It is quiet and less people at home. I can golf here, and I don't need Lake Michigan anymore."

While I myself am so glad that I am alive, I enjoy the kids and their friends. In a few short years, they will not be here to be enjoyed in such uninhibited surroundings. For them, this is young adulthood at its best. How could it be better? They have Lake Michigan, the golf course, campfires at night on the beach with friends, and great restaurants. What more could a college student ask for?

As for myself, I am healing on the inside and the outside. I am also preparing to finish round one and start round two: radiation. Often, I speak on the phone with Jane. She lives in Toledo, Ohio and I live in Holland; so we don't see each other often, but the bond could not be any deeper. There was many a day that notes of treatment were compared. We would share stories about hair, family, husbands, scars, bandages, parties, and treatments. On some days there would be many a tear shed and sometimes belly busting laughter. She has become my twin sister in cancer and life. The blessings are so great.

Yesterday, I went for a ride on Laddie. He has new horse-shoes. His feet are less painful, and he is like riding a Cadillac. I had a quiet day. I lay out in the sun and went to take the two dogs for a walk. Both Pollix and Pumpkin love to walk any-time, but night is the best for them.

Yesterday, I saw my friend Deb. She is a few months ahead of me in cancer treatment. She looks absolutely fantastic. Deb has one week of treatment left; then she will be finished—fin-ished and alive. What a woman. Last weekend, she had a team of friends that went with her and her husband to participate in Relay for Life on her behalf. They collected money and walked the night together as friends to give the donations to cancer research. What a great group of supporting friends and a supporting husband she has.

When I look in the mirror, I still can't believe that it is me looking back. I have no hair anywhere—not even on my legs or eyebrows. I do have two, yes; count them, two eyelashes left that I apply mascara to every day. Why I do this I really am not sure, but I do. I also still have a great smile. How could it be that I could still smile? It is because no matter how awful it gets, I know that my hand is in the hand of God. I need just squeeze to feel it there.

As I look in the mirror, I go through the checklist of what I see: a mother, a wife, an employee, a survivor, a child of God, and a tired old woman with numb fingers and feet. I see scars, no hair, two eyelashes, weight gain, and a smile. On the inside, I still feel beautiful, young, and so full of dreams for the future. How could there be such a contrast?

Sometimes, I could just scream. Can't I just get out of this body for a short time and have a new one, one that doesn't ache? I realize that this is the body that God gave me and I should never complain because God still lets me use it. Hot flashes and all the other excitement it is completely mine. Thank you, God, for life.

Thursday, June 26, 2003
sunny, warm, seventy nine degrees

Today is a perfect Michigan day. My sister from Florida, Erin, came here today. I picked her up from Grand Rapids. My other sister, Claudia, from Maryland is also here with two of her children, Claire and Seth. We all went to lunch; and in the evening, Laurelin and Travis stayed with Claire and Seth while Erin, Claudia, and I went to a beautiful dinner on the lake. Tad had left for the day. Was he golfing or biking?

The three of us went first to a garden walk by Lake Michigan. The home was spectacular, as if a home from a magazine. The gardens were perfectly manicured, and I commented,

"When I have a gardener, I will sit in the garden and paint, not weed." This was met with rounds of gut-breaking laughter and more dialogs about, "When I have ... " We spent hours discussing what we might do at our garden at our homes someday.

Next, we went on to a dinner overlooking a marina on Lake Michigan.

"Are you three related? You look so alike?"

"We are all sisters, and we are here to laugh, enjoy a wonderful meal, and share with one another."

"It has been too long since we were together, with only the three of us."

"Would you three ladies like to sit by the water, overlooking the marina?"

"Yes, we would. We are celebrating *life*."

We shared the most wonderful conversation. Without them, I would have never made it this far. I have called and cried for hours into the phone, just to hear their voices comfort me in my loneliness. We shared stories from the past and life experiences from the present. Both of them asked the question, "Thais, is there anything I can do to make your life easier?"

"Just be there for me as you have. And while you are here, I need lots of hugs."

The evening was winding down at the restaurant, so we left. No. Actually, we were nicely kicked out of the restaurant. To be kicked out when we were having such fun seemed a bit odd. I guess they weren't having as much fun as we were.

We went home and lit the candles on our wraparound porch and opened a bottle of vintage wine. The conversation began to flow into the wee hours of the morning. We shared our hopes and dreams from childhood. We shared those dreams that had been realized and those that had not. We discussed children, the joy and frustration of being a parent. We talked candidly about marriage and the willingness that it takes to surrender your agenda for the other person. If *both* of you are *giving*, the relationship becomes stronger. This is where the chaff is removed and blown into the wind. Sometimes, the relationships cannot withstand the fire of the refiner's oven.

> Under three things the earth trembles, under four it cannot bear up: a servant who becomes a king, a fool who is full of food, an unloved woman who is married, and a maidservant who displaces her mistress.
>
> Proverbs 30:21–23

Friday, June 27, 2003
sunny, warm, gentle breezes

We are up bright and early because Dad and Mom are coming to pick everyone up. Erin and Claudia's families, along with Mom and Dad, will go to Beulah, in Northern Michigan; to spend a few days at the beach. There will then be a celebration of life at a memorial for my aunt and uncle. They had been married since WWII and died within months of each other. God had not given them children, but they led a wonderful life based around God and one another until the end.

I am way too exhausted to go today. Lying and resting on the beach, sounds so good; but I don't think my family knows the word *rest*. Maybe Tad will come with me if I go later. I will go up north in a day or two. There have been so few words said between Tad and I for months now. We used to golf together and go out for a bike ride or dinner together occasionally. We used to attend school functions together, and now none of these things are happening. He seems to want to be in total separation from our family and me. He won't talk to me about any of these concerns. I slipped under Tad's pillow a card that said, "I want you in my life."

Saturday, June 28, 2003
sunny, clear skies, eighty degrees

Today, I left for Beulah by myself. I had asked Tad to come with me more than one time; but Tad had other plans, and it appears that they don't include me.

It was such a nice memorial service commemorating two lives that mirrored each other. Visiting with my relatives, I realized that so many of them are getting older. Last year, it was my grandmother's memorial and the year before, my uncles. The thought crosses my mind, *will I be next? Or will it be my father who fights the results of a severe stroke each and every day? Who will it be? Who is next?* After the memorial, my parents, sisters, brothers, and their families all drove to the north to the villages of Northport, Suttons Bay, Glen Arbor and Traverse City. These are all wonderful little fishing villages, with shopping and hiking trails and great little eateries.

The evening closed with a family dinner at Manitou Inn. This great restaurant is a log home in the northern woods that serves freshly caught fish daily. The night was a memorable one, with laughter and tears from our families and spouses as we shared stories of past and present. We all shared so much love at one table. Again, here I was in a situation that should have been shared with a husband; but again, I realized how alone I am. The family drove the thirty-minute scenic route around Crystal Lake, where my father grew up, and then, at last, to our temporary home: the Pine Knot Motel in Beulah. I believe that this motel has not changed since 1960 and the clock always reads 11:45 at the Pine Knot. It is a place where time has stood still.

Sunday, June 29, 2003
extremely cold and rainy

There were mayflies everywhere on the screens, cars and windows when we awoke in the morning. We walked with our abundant family, our breakfast of pecan muffins and coffee over to the beach at Crystal Lake to experience the sunrise. What an artist God is. It was exceptionally good to be with my family experiencing such morning beauty in the sunrise.

When we arrived at home, Todd, my brother; his wife; and their three children, Mitchell, Mackenzie and Spencer, were waiting on the porch to enjoy dinner tonight with our family. They were unable to go up north because of a work commitment. It was good to have everyone together. There must have been at least eighteen of us, and all able to be accommodated together in our home. The weather was beautiful; and tables were set outdoors on the porch. Yard games were in full play while others of us sat and visited. Matt and Laurelin made a special effort to be there for dinner. Tad was golfing. We all had a fantastic time with joyfulness and laughter, reminiscing of memories of long ago. Daddy and Mom looked so happy. At my home they had four of their five children together and most of their families; and joy showed on their tired faces. The evening was seventy-five degrees with a soft breeze. Lemon smells from the moon flowers in the garden drifted on the breezes as the sun slowly set and music softly played. The late-night good-byes brought tears to my eyes. I know that everyone will return to their lives some hundreds of miles away. Will I ever see them again?

Morning came too quickly. We prepared a great breakfast, and then we were off to the airport with Erin to return to Florida. There were constant tears, and more tears through smiles and great bear hugs. Now they are all gone, and I am left again to myself.

A Silence That Stills My Heart

Thursday, July 24, 2003
blue skies, sunny, seventy five degrees at 8:00 *a.m.*

This is without doubt a glorious day. The white, puffy clouds hang in the sky like giant marshmallows.

My skin screams in pain from the sores. My hands and feet have varying degrees of numbness that is painful, but I now walk with slightly less joint pain due to the steroids that I am taking. I am a person who likes fruits and vegetables and eats organic. No chemicals for me! Now I have to accept chemicals, and lots of them, to stay alive. How ironic.

But today is my *last* chemo day.

I bought blushing pink and ivory roses for Dr. Kindness and Melissa who has held my hand and comforted me on many a day. The wonderful thrill is that the chemo nurses bought *me* flowers. Jeanne came to sit with me and brought a beautiful plant with butterflies for my new beginning away from cancer and treatments. Erin and Claudia sent flowers, and all my family are sending prayers. Matthew came to visit and held my hand if I needed it and gave hugs if necessary. He sat with me, reading to me for a while, before leaving for his shift of work.

Tad had dropped me off and picked me up when I was finished and the office was closing. This chemo is extremely strong, and I felt very tired and out of control when I arrived at home. I wanted to go see my horses because I realized that the day was so beautiful. The reality of it was that I couldn't even stand up straight or say a complete sentence. I was exceedingly tired. I laid down and fell asleep just like they said that I would. I am so powerless over this disease. Where will my power to take this from my body come from?

> To keep me from becoming conceited because of these surpassingly great revelations, there was given me a thorn in my flesh, a messenger of Satan, to torment me. Three times I pleaded to the Lord to take it away from me. But he said to me, "My grace is sufficient for you, for my power is made perfect in weakness." Therefore I will boast all the more gladly about my weakness, so that Christ's power may rest on me. That is why, for Christ's sake, I delight in weaknesses, in insults, in hardships, in persecutions, in difficulties. For when I am weak, I am strong.
>
> 2 Corinthians 12:7–10

Wednesday, July 30, 2003

Back to work today. It is hard to believe that this is *my* body that I am walking around in. Every part and inch of this body is painful. My fingers and feet are numb, and my skin is immensely sore. My hair is at best fuzzy and gray. My thoughts are not complete unless I stop and think about tying them all together. The numbness seems overwhelming at times. I shuffle when I walk. There is such great pain in my joints, even with the steroids that are helping decrease the pain. A human hug would be so greatly desired and appreciated, the contact of a person that loved me in spite of all that my body has been through. Please, dear God, I would so appreciate a little human contact.

Tad says again, "I cannot hug you." What about that vow "in sickness and in health?" He got the "in health" part very well but has decided that the "in sickness" part didn't apply to him. When I ask, "Can you explain this to me?" He throws up his hands into the air and walks away. Can you take one half of a wedding vow? Is it a legal marriage? Can you only take the vows of the marriage that you want to, only the vows that make you happy, only the vows that serve your needs? I don't think that this is what God had in mind when he brought a man and a woman together.

A dear, joyful friend of mine, Skip, died a few days ago, only hours after I saw him happy and joyful, full of smiles and conversation at a jazz concert. Skip passed unto the Lord on Tad's birthday. He was found in his bed, no longer breathing. He had died in his sleep of a sudden and massive heart attack. He was taken by the angels, I am sure. He was the kind of man that everyone wanted to be near. He always made each person feel as though they were the only person who mattered in this world at the moment when he spoke with you. He will be greatly missed by many.

Yesterday, my Mom and Dad bought cemetery plots. Tomorrow will be one year since Daddy's stroke. I think every day he envisions having another. He has not regained movement and the ability to walk well at all. He struggles each day with physical therapy and speech, but the body is failing; and he knows it.

He has told me that at night, sometimes he dreams that he is healthy and I and my four brothers and sisters are all at home. He is playing ball with us in the yard running and laughing. "Thais, I could move for hours, effortlessly and joyfully, moving without pain or difficulty." In the dreams, he spoke to each of us children with no loss of words, with complete and total ease of communication. Then he awakes and realizes that it is only a dream, a moment that God gave him to be free of the bonds of the body he now lives in. It was only a dream. Dad and Mom have worked so hard to be the new normal.

This all makes me think about when I will die. Someday, we all will die. I believe that I am ready to meet my Lord God. If I have a choice in the matter, I am not ready to give up my life on earth yet. I feel like I have been placed here to help someone else. Cancer is not fun, but I can't quit yet. I feel that God has another plan for me. I'm not sure what it is, but I must work hard to stay alive now.

Now I rely on my animals who give me great pleasure with unconditional love. My husband is never close enough to give me any pleasure, reassurance, or love. Tad has been at the beach cottage these last three days by himself. He said he needed some time alone and didn't want anyone with him. He should be home in a day or two. He pretty much comes and goes as he pleases, with no regard as to what might work for anyone else. Tad has his own agenda.

Saturday, August 2, 2003
hot, sunny, eighty degrees

Today in the afternoon was our friend Skip's funeral. What an awesome man he was. The funeral was at our church in Harbert. Many people attended, and the service was excellent. A few things of Skip's were up front, such as a trombone, golf clubs, and a picture of the family—simple and joyful, just like Skip. After the memorial there was a great party at the country club with many remembrances of him. It all seemed very strange and surreal without Skip's robust laughter. This man will be greatly missed and has lived his life on earth to its fullest.

> You see that his faith and his actions are working together, and his faith was made complete by what he did. And the scripture was fulfilled that says, "Abraham believed God, and it was credited to him as righteousness," and he was called God's friend. You see that a person is justified by what he does and not by faith alone.
>
> James 2:22–24

Saturday night

It has taken much courage to get to this night. It is my thirty year class reunion tonight. I have gone to every reunion that we have had in thirty years. This one is different. Even if I lose weight, buy new clothes, or do any other thing that a woman does to look good to her old classmates, I still have cancer. I may never be alive for another reunion. But today I have no hair, no eyebrows, and scars everywhere on my body. Should I go or not? I will talk with God about this one. I read:

> I sought the Lord and he heard me, and delivered me from all my fears. Those who look to him are radiant; their faces are never covered with shame. This poor man called, and the LORD heard him; he saved him out of all of his troubles. The angel of the LORD encamps around those who fear him, and he delivers them.
>
> Psalm 34:4–7

I wasn't going to go tonight; but after I opened my Bible and Psalm 34 stared at me, I figured it was a sign from God to go. I became calm. At the last minute, Laurelin talked me into it. "Mom, wear the long, sexy, auburn wig, the *fun* hair and no one will know that you don't have hair. Mom, it is so you and *you are beautiful.*" It was confirmed by Matt, from school, that the auburn wig, the *fun* hair, was the way to go. What would I do without these two gifts from God? Laurelin said, "I will be your makeup artist." My greatest fear had been that I would be dancing wildly, enjoying myself, feeling no pain, and this was when my beautiful, long, sexy, auburn hair might fly off my head and into a classmate's arms. Can you imagine the horror?

My friend, Deb that is only months ahead of me in cancer treatments offered her wig tape. I have never heard of such a thing. Tonight I will give my fears to God and enjoy old friends.

Trembling but strong, I walked into the restaurant; head held high, I realized that these were my friends. Tad had decided to come at the last minute and was by my side. Lately, Tad had taken no interest in going anywhere with me, so I found it very unusual that he would come to my class reunion. Laurelin's and Matthew's voices were in my mind, saying, "Way to go, Mom. Walk tall. I am so proud of you!" It was a wonderful reunion to see old friends that are all getting old just like me. Without the name tags that had senior high school pictures on them, I am not sure that I could have recognized many of the people. I would sometimes turn to a friend and say, "Do we know the man or the woman of that couple"; and they would turn and say, "I have no idea who that is!"

The dancing was awesome, and the tape worked well to hold on my wig. Compliments were flying about how my hair was as beautiful as it was in high school; and the wig held tight to the smooth, bald head underneath. By the end of the night, I had taken my wig off so many times to show those friends that were closest to me in school that I was bald I had lost count. I had to say over and over again to them, "Yes, I really do have cancer and no hair." The gasps and the hands running over my soft, bald skin were numerous. These friends from thirty years ago were offering me support as a survivor and confirming in my mind that I wasn't a freak. They offered more support with their kind words than Tad had over these months of treatment. Of course, I didn't remove my wig on the dance floor; so many people still had no idea that I was a cancer survivor.

I had to catch up with all of the adventures that we had experienced in the last five years. Tongues were flapping. "How are the children and where are they?" Discussions about how many grandchildren were in their lives and how old. I asked if anyone had heard about my boyfriend, Terry, of three years in high school. It was very unusual that he and his wife, Lora, of many years weren't there. His children were about as old as mine, and we had always caught up on family and friends at these reunions.

In high school, he had been my best friend. We had grown up in each other's arms and each other's lives for years. We experienced the first kiss, first car, first drive-in, first argument, and the deepest bonding of two souls that could happen in high school. He knew everything about me, and I knew everything about him. We had experienced life in high school and outside of class while we skipped class to tan at the beach and go to Indiana for lunch. We were out of school for any reason that we could think of to be out of class.

We both knew that we couldn't marry but that we would be best friends until death; we had an extremely deep bond. While I was remembering all of this, my classmate brought me back to life with the words, "He died recently of cancer." I was rudely and abruptly transported back to earth. Died? As in no longer alive? How could he have died? He was young! He was my age! I have cancer and I haven't died. Why is he not alive?

He was my best friend, the person who I shared everything with. How could he no longer be on this earth? *Cancer!* I hate that word! In the past, after high school, he wrote me a letter about us growing up and about how much he appreciated our friendship at that very difficult time in our lives. I thought it unusual that he wrote that letter; but I felt the same, so I just held it dear to my heart. Did he know then that he had cancer? Was it his way of closing anything in his life that may not have been said or written to others?

He was dead due to cancer? Somehow I just couldn't comprehend that it was possible. I will have to make sure of this. I know that cancer only wins if you don't have God in your life. With God, you *live* after you die. It is like a promotion that will be an *eternity*, not just a lifetime. Death just seems so final for us here on earth. I will pray for his soul and his family, who loved him very much.

Then I heard a voice from heaven say:

> "Write: Blessed are the dead who die in the Lord from now on." "Yes," says the Spirit, "they will rest from their labor, for their deeds will follow them."
>
> Revelation 14:13

Thursday, August 7, 2003
hot, hot, hot, clear skies

Today is my date to be tattooed for the radiation that I need to receive. I will be having forty-plus treatments in consecutive days. It will equal two months of treatments. The reason that I need to be tattooed my doctor, Dr. Compassion explains, "Is so that they will know where the radiation beam is to be pointed. To be sure the beam is at the correct angle, a tattoo is placed there." I told the technician that was assisting me, "If I have to get a tattoo, I am negotiating for a dolphin or a scorpion." Abruptly, the technician erupted with uncontrollable laughter. "Thais, this is not a tattoo parlor. We specialize in dots and dots only." "Oh!" "These dots must be placed on the exact area of your body that the radiation beam will penetrate. It only takes a few dots." Mine must be placed on my front and back and one other area. It takes about forty-five minutes of complete non-movement to have all areas of your body marked properly. If an area is incorrectly marked, the beam could cause severe damage to the lungs, heart, or other internal organs. More damage is something that I don't need to happen in my life today. To be completely still for forty-five minutes is a long time. All of a sudden, you may have to cough, clear your throat, and scratch a spot on your body. Forty-five minutes is a long time to think about life and death.

It is too much time to think of all of the things that you have accomplished in your life, all those things you had wished you had accomplished, and all the things you may not ever be able to accomplish now that you have cancer. Forty-five minutes is a long time to hold your body and mind still—a very long time. I again am so tired that if my mind was quiet I would fall asleep on the table and rest for forty-five minutes. I laid quietly, in a very awkward position, and felt the grace of God encompass me. Then forty-five long minutes were bearable.

Saturday, August 16, 2003
sunny, hot, and very humid

This is an important day. I shot a 39 on the front nine with Tad at Chikaming Country Club. A thirty nine:————- 4 6 4 5 4 3 5 3 5. Unbelievable! It must be all those steroids to prevent the pain in my joints. This is the first time I have ever shot so low of a score. It was effortless. Then we stopped for lunch, and the game left as easily as it came. What a thrill that was!

We drove over to Mom and Dad's to help with work at the house. It is just too hard for Mom and Dad to do work around the house since Dad's stroke. Laurelin should be home soon from her trip with Travis's family to Canada. She will have her biopsy for cancer on Monday. Oh, dear God, please let her have no cancer. Give it to me instead.

Monday, August 18, 2003
hot, humid, sunny, big white clouds roll in the sky

Today, my daughter underwent a biopsy for cancer. I am exhausted with worry and with pain from the physical trauma that my body has undergone trying to kill the cancer in me. I am also working my full-time schedule so I can pay the bills that Tad thinks I am responsible for. His statement in June, "Don't worry about the money..." didn't last long. Laurelin, Travis, and I were at the hospital by 7:00 a.m. Travis and I waited with Laurelin for her appointed time. Travis was very comforting and tender with Laurelin. Laurelin and I were glad that he was there. He held Laurelin's hand, stroked her hair, and reminded her that she was in God's hands. Travis, with a kind, warm human heart and hand, was there to ease her through her possible doubts or fears. I did wish so much that I could have played out that scene with Tad. No, mine had been a completely different scene. The nurse came into our area and in a happy voice said, "It is your turn, Laurelin." She waved as they wheeled her away.

God, I am not sure how much more *I* can take. I moved off to an area to be by myself to talk with God. *My faith is stronger each day that I rely on you. Please, I don't think I could still function if I knew that Laurelin had cancer. I realize that you do already know the outcome of this biopsy, but please let this biopsy for my daughter be negative. Please!* In the Bible, it says that we should ask for what we need, as children ask their parents. I always thought that if I prayed for something for myself that it was selfish. *Now, God, after reading your book more often, I know differently.*

Travis and I were waiting when Laurelin came from surgery still asleep. Tad came in about then and stayed until she awoke. The biopsy won't be back for a few days. Again, it will be just a few more days of waiting and not knowing the end result. Trust, faith, and patience.

> Rejoice in the Lord always, I will say it again: Rejoice! Let your gentleness be evident to all. The Lord is near. Do not be anxious about anything, but in everything, by prayer and petition, with thanksgiving, present your requests to God. And the peace of God, which transcends all understanding, will guard your hearts and your minds in Christ Jesus.
>
> Philippians 4:4–7

God, I pray for comfort for our minds that race all too fast about the worrying. You have shown me in the Bible that it says that worrying will not add one hour to my life. Please bring comfort in waiting these few days. The doctor said that the biopsy will be back in three days. Is that not how long it was before Jesus was raised from the dead?

As we leave the hospital, I remembered that Travis's grandmother is in coma at a hospital and will soon be taken off the ventilator. Maybe today? She will then pass away sometime soon, for her body can no longer support itself. She is a woman of God and will assuredly be sitting with God in heaven. God must be so busy taking care of us all of the time.

Khanada was sick this morning. I gave her Banamine to help with the stomachache that she was having. I prayed that she would be comfortable because I had to take Laurelin for the biopsy. I have had to leave this whole day in God's hands. Isn't that what I am supposed to do every day? Why do I always think that I can control all of the situations? When the going gets tough, then I call God in. I really don't think that is what he wants me to do. I should talk with him daily and ask his guidance daily—hourly if need be—instead of asking after I have messed up the situation. When will this earthly child ever learn?

Tad went back to work after Laurelin awoke in the hospital. We went home for us to all rest after the surgery. Laurelin was a bit affected by the anesthetic still and couldn't be left alone. Travis was a great doctor, taking care of all of her needs.

He made sure that she was warm enough, had enough pillows, and had a drink if she needed it. He stayed by her side as she fell to sleep.

Again, I am just exhausted. I was up too early and have been worrying too much. I am trying to prepare my body and mind for radiation treatments after I work all day tomorrow. I went out to check my horse, and the person who cared for the horses was mucking out stalls. I asked if Khanada seemed as though she had been in any distress. He said, "She seemed fine." To me, she was a little too quiet. I have seen this in her before, and it was not a good thing. I gave her more medicine and stayed for awhile. Khanada didn't seem in great distress, just uncannily quiet; so I walked home. Travis and Laurelin were quietly resting, so I lay down for a short nap.

The doorbell rang franticly at 7:00 p.m. and woke me from a very deep sleep. When I opened the door, my friend stood there. She also boards her horse with mine at the barn behind my home. She looked extremely distressed. She said that my horse had been sweating, rolling, pounding, and thrashing on the ground so hard that she had made a complete cake of mud over her entire body. My horse was in acute distress. This was severe colic. This was *not* good.

I ran out to check her with my bare head and no wig. She needed a vet, pronto. The phone in the barn didn't work, and Tad had thought for months that I didn't need a cell phone. I had to run home to use the phone and wait until a call was returned to me from my vet. Fortunately, these vets are the best; but their location is a least forty-five minutes away. The call was returned quickly, and I was advised to use the extremely strong pain killer that I had been given for just such an emergency. I was to put her in the stall and inject her. The vet explained that Khanada would rest until she could get there in about forty-five minutes to one hour.

I walked into and through the barn to the pasture. Khanada was in great pain—head pitching left to right, feet pounding, and with the most intense whinny I had ever heard. I tried to get her into a stall so I could give the injection. She was frantic because Laddie, her pasture mate of ten years, was still in the pasture. I had to capture and halter Laddie and then bring him into the barn. The whites of his eyes were showing, ears were pinned back, and he was loudly whinnying. He looked scared to death. With Laddie inside, he became a bit less frantic. Khanada was frantic also until she saw Laddie; then she settled down.

I took the needle cap off and gave a prayer that she would stand still with the great pain she was in while I gave the injection. She stopped moving and looked me straight in the eye while I gave the injection. Within one minute, my beautiful, white thoroughbred mare that had carried me over hills, valleys, jumps, and creeks had collapsed on the stall floor.

She appeared to not be breathing; and her gums were very gray in color, which usually means shock. I stood and waited a moment. Why I waited a moment, and for what, I am not sure. I suppose I waited a moment so my mind could clear to make the next decision. Was she dead or resting?

Other boarders that had come for a peaceful ride on their horses and the owners of the barn stood and stared in great shock. I don't believe that any of them had seen anything like this before. I couldn't do anything now. I ran back home at about 8:oo p.m. to call my vet and tell her what had happened. The vet explained that she may be in a deep sleep. I was to just let her rest. Dr. Rubie explained that to the contrary of many people's thinking, walking was *not* what she needed now.

When I returned, the gawkers had decided that she needed to get up so that she did not die in the stall. They were pulling on her with the lead rope and kicking her to make her stand. I absolutely shouted in anger, "Stop and leave, all of you! This is not what she needs now. The vet will be here soon." I realized at that moment that she most likely would have to be put to sleep when the vet came. At this point, I had an extremely sick horse that had been nothing but kind to me; and she was being kicked and beaten.

My daughter was resting at home with Travis. Travis's grandmother who has been fighting her own battle may be taken off life support today. I will be starting my radiation tomorrow after working the entire day. I have just finished six months of chemo therapy. This, I realized, was major crisis management. My husband sat in the house and read the newspaper while I dealt with all this by myself.

Some of the people left the barn, and I ran home to make another call. Why does everyone but me have a cell phone? I explained to Laurelin what the situation was. "Khanada will most likely have to be put to sleep tonight." Laurelin was not sure if she wanted to be there or not. I walked back out to the barn with a heavy heart and what felt like a ball and chain wrapped around my ankles. So many things had taken place these last few days.

I walked into Khanada's stall. Her eyes were open, and she looked at me. She was exhausted and full of sweat and mud. Her white fur was a multitude of colors of brown, and tears streamed from her eyes. I whispered to her and gently stroked her long neck and soft muzzle.

Khanada was the animal that I have had to share my life with on a daily basis because my husband couldn't deal with my cancer. How did my sickness affect him? I have had more hours spent in conversation and tears with this animal than my husband. This animal was always there for me. She knew when I was sad. She would so often wrap that big neck and body around me until my sobbing would stop. She was always there for me, always. Some nights, the sadness was so great at home between Tad and me that I would go out to the barn and sleep next to her the entire night. Tad never even knew or cared that I was gone, and now this friend that had helped me to have the will to live was dying.

Tad surprised me and came out to the barn. He found me in Khanada's stall, stroking her neck. "She looks like a dying horse." He continued, "Laurelin says that if you have to put Khanada to sleep, she wants to be there. Come and get her."

He left, and I sobbed and sobbed. This time, I was holding Khanada, and she rested quietly in *my* arms. Soon, Dr Rubie, my vet, came. She is a great vet and an awesome woman and friend. I was so glad it was Dr Rubie that was on call. God had answered my prayer. I coaxed Khanada into finally standing. She was very unsteady, and Laddie was constantly whinnying. Khanada's exam was completed, and the diagnosis was in. She lay back down, exhausted. My Khanada could not be saved. She had to be euthanized before the pain became greater.

With a heavy heart, I had walked home to talk with Laurelin. She was not feeling well herself but wanted to be there, for she had also loved Khanada. I slowly walked back to the barn.

When I arrived at her stall, I tenderly talked to Khanada. I ran my hand gently and slowly over her forehead and neck. Eventually she was able to, with great difficulty, get up and come with me out of the barn and onto the dirt drive. I knew that after death the rendering truck could pick her up from here. I whispered to Khanada, and she stood quietly and nuzzled into my neck. Her fur, although full of mud, was so soft in places; and she smelled so good. I thought it very unusual that it was such a perfect summer's night, for now it was midnight. How could this beautiful night hold such tenderness and such sadness all at the same time?

Laurelin and Travis came out to the barn. Laurelin stroked Khanada and softly spoke to her. Laurelin's eyes filled with tears, and this brought more sadness to my heart. We both took a few minutes to tell Khanada that there was no other option and that we loved her with all of our hearts. She had been such a good horse, a dream and prayer come true for two redheads from Michigan.

The vet said tenderly, "It is now time."

As the injection was given, Khanada looked at us as if to say she understood. It took about five seconds, and she dropped gracefully to her knees and quietly lay down as if to sleep at my feet.

Within seconds, she was gone; and the magnitude of the beauty of the night shook me. It was a warm, quiet evening with millions of brilliant stars in God's heaven. There was a soft breeze with a crescent moon hanging in the sky. The crickets kept right on chirping, even though one of my best friends had just died.

Laurelin and Travis, both exhausted, went home. Laurelin wasn't feeling well, and this had just added more anguish to her. What was there to stay for? Khanada had died. Dr Rubie and I stayed for awhile, sitting by Khanada's head. I was stroking her fur while Dr. Rubie and I talked, remembering when I first asked her to examine this beautiful white horse that was for sale.

As I stroked Khanada's neck, she felt so warm and soft. This animal that I had shared so much of my life with was gone forever. Does God have room in heaven for our animals? Dr Rubie left at about 1:30 a.m. God could not have sent a more caring person to put my animal to sleep and comfort me.

I have survived cancer, surgeries, treatments, my daughter's cancer biopsy, my father's stroke, and now the loss of

Khanada and a husband that doesn't care about the sorrow because it is not his. God, I know that you have asked me to have great endurance. I tell you tonight that I feel I can bear no other sadness at this time. My endurance is at the end. I do not believe that I can take any more.

Now everyone had gone, and I was alone with Khanada. I prayed on my knees there and then that my daughter's biopsy would be negative and that God would give me more endurance and perseverance at that minute. It was 3:00 a.m., and I needed to be awake in three hours to prepare for work. I stopped, covered Khanada, and closed a chapter in my life. *My heart was still.*

> Consider it pure joy, my brothers, whenever you face trials of many kinds, because you know that the resting of your faith develops perseverance. Perseverance must finish its work so that you may be mature and complete, not lacking anything. If any of you lacks wisdom, he should ask God, who gives generously to all without finding fault, and it will be given to him. But when he asks, he must believe and not doubt, because he who doubts is like a wave of the sea, blown and tossed by the wind. That man should not think he should receive anything from the Lord; he is a double minded man, unstable in all he does.
>
> James 1:2–8

> We did not want you to be uninformed, brothers, about the hardships we suffer in the province of Asia. We were under great pressure, far beyond our ability to endure, so that we despaired even of life. Indeed in our hearts we felt the sentence of death. But this happened so that we might not rely on ourselves but on God, who raises the dead. He has delivered us from such a deadly peril, and he will deliver us. On him we have set our hope that he will continue to deliver us, as you help us by our prayers.
>
> 2 Corinthians 1:8–11

Dear God, Help Me through All This!

I always thought that it was selfish to ask God for help. But I have learned differently. God wants us to pray to him daily and ask for his help. I also remember in the Bible, David saying, "Wait for the LORD; be strong and take heart and wait for the LORD" (Psalm 27:14).

The men of the Bible who followed God daily sometimes would wait days or years before God answered their prayers. Then, many times, it would not be the answer that they looked for. God always knows best. Like a friend once said, "Sometimes I think that God doesn't give us more than one instruction at a time because he knows that we as humans would try to improve upon the ultimate perfect plan that God has for our lives."

Dear friends, if our hearts do not condemn us, we have confidence before God and receive from him anything we ask; because we obey his commands and do what pleases him. And this is his command: to believe in the name of his Son, Jesus Christ, and to love one another as he commanded us. Those who obey his commands live in him, and he in them. And this is how we know that he lives in us: We know it by the spirit he gave us.

1 John 3:21–24

For everyone that asks receives; he who seeks finds; and to him who knocks, the door will be opened. Ask and it will be given to you; seek and you will find; knock and the door will be opened for you.

Matthew 7:7–8

Tuesday, August 19, 2003
6:00 a.m., sunny, hot already

Dear God, we need to have a talk now. Please! My body is falling apart, my family is falling apart, and my marriage is falling apart. I know that you have something much greater than this in store for me. I feel like Job when God said to Satan, "Have you considered my servant, Job?" (Job1:8) I also think of Joseph, who endured so much. Then there was Paul, who learned to be content in any situation. Can you give me their faith and strength? If I leave a paper and pen, will you write me a letter and tell me what to do and where to go in my life? I know that you are with me or I would not be able to endure these trials, but I need some guidance, some rest from these trials.

I believe that to trust is the key, but please give me the strength. Job, Paul, and Joseph's stories are in my heart; but I know their outcomes. They trusted not knowing what you had in store for them. Please give me the strength or come to me in a dream and make clear the plans you have for me. I must trust, trust always. That means no matter what. Okay. I understand you are telling me to trust. But just in case you have a little extra time tonight to write it all down, my instructions for my life, I will leave you a big note pad and a pen.

It is a quiet and still 6:00 am. It is time to get out of bed and start another day. I am on overload and exhausted. I have had only two hours of sleep, and I need to get to work. I walked out to the barn to see my lifeless Khanada for the last time and to see how Laddie was doing. I removed the tarp from Khanada; she looked like she was quietly and peacefully asleep.

Soon, the truck would be backing up to take away the body of this horse that had been the answer to so many dreams; this friend, this animal who helped me get through so much of my cancer and treatments when my husband was not willing to give any comfort.

Laddie is dreadfully confused and he whinnies, stomps, paces, and pounds on the dirt. He is very upset. He and Khanada have been together for years and years. He too has lost a friend.

I am exhausted as I go to work. I work, praying hourly that Laurelin's biopsy is negative. We will find out tomorrow. *Trust,* it is only five letters, but it is a big word. Work was long, and radiation seemed even longer. When will my life be whole again?

Wednesday, August 20, 2003
hot, dry, windy, ninety degrees

I went out to see Laddie. He is very quiet. He now also has an infection and he needs antibiotics two times daily. I have the afternoon off because I have follow-up chemo blood work and I will go to radiation again. I also have a doctor's appointment and errands to run. Again, I am exhausted. I have too many places that I have to be in one day. Do these people not know that there is only one of me?

Laurelin's doctor called and spoke with me at 5:30 p.m. The biopsy was *not* cancer. My response was a dance of joy, jubilation, happiness, and exhaustion. This had been the answer to my prayers. Thank you, God! On my knees, I gave praises and more praises.

Thursday, August 21, 2003
hot, not so humid, beautiful day, eighty degrees

Laddie is extremely lonely and very quiet. His infection is getting worse. Can a horse have a broken heart? He won't eat, and he just stands in the same place all day long. I went out to talk with him, stroke his long back, and brush him.

Laurelin starts college in a few days, and she also is extremely quiet. She is in pain from the biopsy that they had to take. She may be concerned about starting school or meeting a new roommate. She is wondering who will take care of me if I need help once she is gone. I will greatly miss Laurelin, all of her help and her hugs.

Saturday, August 23, 2003
sunny, seventy five degrees

Laddie seemed possibly a little better today. This brings joy to my tired heart. My Mom and Dad and Mrs. Marschke, Mom's lifelong friend, came to visit me. They are so good to me and know how to raise my spirits, each brought wonderful gifts. I feel honored that they would care about me and take the time to come and visit. Then I was off to see Laurelin for a family picnic at her new home away from home, Hope College. I miss her so much but do want her to begin to establish a life of her own.

Sunday, August 24, 2003
sunny, seventy degrees

Today was a church service at the Hope Chapel. It was very crowded and a beautiful service. Afterward, Tad, Laurelin, Travis, Matt, Alli, and I walked over to brunch at the Alpine Rose restaurant.

After a wonderful brunch Tad wanted to bike ride alone, again. I went home, walked out to the barn and had an amazing ride on Laddie. He seems to miss me more now that Khanada is gone when I don't see him every day.

I lay down in the grass while Laddie grazed around me and I watched the clouds. This was something I could spend hours doing in the yard on a summer's day as a little girl. In these clouds, I was always looking for turtles, dogs, kittens, and dragons that breathed fire.

This was one of those perfect Michigan days: sunny, about seventy to eighty degrees with a teasing wind that could ruffle your hair, if you have any, the bluest sky that you could ever imagine, and white puffy clouds floating effortlessly overhead and constantly changing shapes. I was able to relax and enjoy all of the beauty created for me by God in this one place on earth. I was completely in awe.

As I was looking at the clouds, it crossed my mind that maybe one of the clouds was forming into a white shape that I was so familiar with. This cloud looked like Khanada, galloping across the sky in all of her grandeur. Khanada's head was held high with pride, her long mane caressed her neck as her tail flowed wildly in the wind. She had a majestic command of the skies. This cloud floated in shape above my head for what seemed like hours. I had time to think of the wonderful places this horse had taken my daughter and myself. I had a chance to relive my conversations with this horse during all of my cancer treatments and surgeries. These thoughts floated through my mind, and some not without heartache.

I turned to look at Laddie, and he had stopped eating and was just looking at the ground where Khanada loved to graze. I reached for his muzzle to give him a pet and saw a small area of four-leaf clovers below where he was looking. This had always been Khanada's favorite place to graze. I looked to the heavens to see the horse cloud one more time, and it was gone. Four-leaf clovers and a whole patch of them lay beneath Laddie's muzzle. Assuredly, things would be better. It was a sign. Correct?

Matt is leaving Tuesday for college. I will miss his help and his great hugs.

I will miss my children. I will be on my own now.

Tuesday, August 26, 2003
hot, humid, rain in the forecast

The accumulation of radiation treatment, along with the chemo, my daughter's cancer biopsy, the death of my beautiful horse, and kids leaving for college is taking its toll on me. Yesterday, I came home from work and slept from 7:00 p.m. to 7:00 a.m. without interruption.

Today, I had to work, so Tad went with Matt to get him moved into his new apartment at Western Michigan University. Tonight, after work, I came home and gave Laddie his medicine. He is exceptionally quiet. He needs a little fun in his life—maybe a new pasture mate. He has been with Khanada for over ten years, turned out in pastures daily together. Now he has no other horses with him. I will see about getting him a new buddy for turnout in the pasture.

Then I came home, walked in, and placed my keys on the counter. The silence was deafening. Tad was not home. It was very still in our home with no children. My children aren't here, and all of their friends and shoes and laughter are also gone. Just quiet, deathly quiet. I'm not sure that I like this very much. There is no one, not one person in this large home to give me a hug or a smile.

Wednesday, September 3, 2003
sunny, eighty degrees

What beautiful white clouds. Laddie's infection is better, but I fear that his heart is not. Tomorrow, from the other six horses that are boarded at this barn, we will find a suitable new pasture mate to be turned out with Laddie.

I am now almost finished with one half of my radiation. The doctor had said that I would be extremely tired and would most likely have burns where the beams hit my skin. They actually know what they are talking about. Why am I always so positive that I will be the exception to the rule? My skin is sore, burned, and beginning to open and bleed; but I look on the bright side. I only have thirty-three days more to do this.

The doctor offered some new soothing cream with the instruction of placing it on all areas at least two to three times a day. How will I apply it to my back? So far, my back has not started to bleed; it's just red and blistered like a terrible sunburn. It does hurt; and Tad does not want to be within ten feet of me, which only increases the pain in my heart. If I have a shirt on, you can't even see the burns on my skin. He treats me as if I am a leper. So applying cream to skin where I cannot reach to prevent burns will not happen.

Boy, if he thinks it is bad from his view, he should be walking in *my* shoes. I am still working four days a week to pay the bills. My patients at work keep me going with all of their notes, calls, prayers and voices of concern.

The office that I work for has been good about letting me take a half hour longer lunch so that I can have radiation treatments everyday. Not much time to eat my lunch except in the car to and from treatment. My co-workers are always offering positive words, stories, and deeds of hope to get me through each day.

Tad won't help put the cream on my skin to prevent the burns from increasing where I can't reach. The nurses at radiation apply it for me after treatment, and the girls at work help apply it first thing in the morning before we see patients. These dear friends do not want me to have any more pain or blistering on my radiation sites than what I already do. I'm in desperation at night because of the pain of the burns, and have spent hours looking through my long-handled kitchen utensils. I have looked for something that I could use by myself to help apply the cream to my back. Finally, I found one that would help aid me. In the evening, I have been applying the cream to a spatula and trying to get it on the sore area of my back. It doesn't work well, but it is better than having no cream applied anywhere. I can only say that necessity is the mother of invention. Maybe I have a new multimillion-dollar idea there.

I know that God has a great plan for me. God has told me many a time in dreams that my job now is to stay alive. Stay alive for what? In the Bible, when God gives a command, he does not give a complete synopsis of what the person is to do. He does not tell the outcome of the actions that he desires. As a human being, our choice is to not have faith or have faith that God will give one command after another. Our tendency as human is; we want to know the entire plan, the whole picture of what we are getting into before the first step is taken. God doesn't work that way. He gives us a command and we are supposed to follow in faith that the final outcome will be what God had planned for our life.

In Acts 8:26–30, Philip trusted that God would give him the commands one at a time to complete God's purpose for Philip in that situation. Philip picked up and left where he was and did as God commanded. I can picture me saying, "Wait, God. I have to pack. God, how long will I be gone? Who will do my job while I am gone? God, what food should I take? Are my sandals going to wear out?" The best one is, "God, are you sure that you have the right person for this job? Isn't someone else more qualified? Is my faith as strong as Philip's?" I only hear, *Thais, you are to heal.* Then what? Please give me Philip's faith.

> Now an angel of the LORD said to Philip, "Go south to the road-the desert road-that goes down to Jerusalem to Gaza." So he started out, and on his way he met an Ethiopian eunuch, an important official that was in charge of all of the treasury of Candace, queen of the Ethiopians. This man had gone to Jerusalem to worship and on his way home was sitting in his chariot reading the book of Isaiah the prophet. The spirit told Philip, "Go to that chariot and stay near it." Then Philip ran up to the chariot and heard the man reading Isaiah the prophet. "Do you understand what you are reading?" Philip asked. "How can I," he said, "unless someone explains it to me.?" So he invited Philip to come up and sit with him.
>
> Acts 8:26–31

This is a possible way that the good news of Christ was spread. Did Philip say, "God, how long will I walk on that road?" or, "God, I can't go now. I have laundry to do"? When the spirit asked Philip to go and stand by that chariot, did Philip say, "Why? What am I to do there?" No. He just trusted with his faith that what God told him to do was the correct thing to do—no questions; no buts, ands, or what ifs. He never said, "God, what if I don't have time to do this?" He displayed three things: *trust, faith, and obedience.*

Please, dear God, give me the strength of Philip when I hear your command and to not question but to obey. Teach me to know, it is your will for me. My command from God has been, "Heal now, Thais, for I have something greater than cancer in store for your life." I hear you saying, "Heal on the inside and outside." These simple words from God I hear: "Thais, have trust, faith, obedience, and hope, no matter how difficult it gets. I am with you."

My body is sore where I now have radiation burns, but the radiation is killing the cancer. How lucky that I have cancer now instead of forty years ago. My hair? The best word to describe it is *fuzzy*, like a tennis ball with a salt and pepper overtone. That description is much different than bald as a cue ball, and vastly different than the beautiful auburn that it was. But it is my hair, part of a new beginning. I am nearing the end of treatment, so I can have a new beginning to life.

Saturday, September 6, 2003
sunny, warm, eighty degrees

I slept twelve hours last night and never woke up until morning. Today, I went for a ride on Laddie. We need each other so much now. I am glad that I still have him. His infection seems much better, but he is still extraordinarily quiet. Please let his infection leave him. If this infection gets worse, he will also have to be euthanized. Please let it be gone soon.

I picked up Laurelin from college to come home for dinner. She filled us in on all of the information that is new about school, roommates, and classes. Laurelin really does enjoy Hope College. I took her back, and I am going to bed now at 9:30 p.m. I am sure that I will sleep the entire night. This week, I will be working four days, and radiation is every day this week. I need to keep up my strength.

Sunday, September 7, 2003
hot, sunny, not much wind, eighty degrees

It will be another beautiful day and it could be a warm one by the end of the day. I awoke at 9:30 a.m. My cat was using me as a trampoline.

Matt and his girlfriend came home for dinner. I always love seeing the children at home. Sundays are usually our day to have dinner together. Conversation abounds, and schedules are made for the week. All of us together at one table under one roof. Often, there is laughter, stories, and sharing the past week.

My hands and feet are so numb, even still, after chemotherapy has stopped. I am taking various medications and daily doing exercises that might help correct the problem. I guess I can figure that it is little to pay in pain, time, and money to still be alive.

Saturday, September 13, 2003
partly cloudy, very humid, eighty degrees

Today is my friend's son's wedding. He is twenty years old, just twenty years old. I did that at twenty. I'm not sure at this point in my life if it was the correct thing to do. I am now spending my life going through treatment for my cancer and helping my father after his stroke and treatment, living in a home with the man I married. Twenty-eight years ago he said, "For richer or poorer, and in sickness and in health, until death do us part." Today he has no idea what the health of his family is.

It must be that those vows wear out, become null and void after so many years. Maybe that is why people renew their vows; maybe it isn't a dumb idea after all. I know that it would be easier to live in a home where you didn't expect anyone to be there for you because there just wasn't anyone else in your life. It would be easier than to live in a home where your husband is so detached from you that he has no idea what is going on in your life. It is so emotionally painful. The daily pain I have from cancer treatment is small compared to the pain that my heart feels. Truly, cancer sucks. I have treatment burns, itching, and my skin is peeling. I have no hair, many scars, and deep exhaustion. Would I feel exceedingly less physically painful if I had a mate that was compassionate and could show empathy? Tad has not wanted to go to any counseling and when I ask why he is so distant he turns away. I have asked to his face if he is interested in someone else and he turns and walks away mumbling, "No." All this while trying to continue working and being a mother and wife, and I am in pain most of the time. Yet, the greatest pain is in my heart.

Tad has gone to two sessions with me to a counselor who deals with marriage and the effects of cancer on relationships. He stopped going after those two sessions. His reasoning was, "I am fine." He suggested that I could continue counseling, "Because it seems to be your problem." The counselor didn't see it that way. At this time I will try to survive the cancer and when I am healthy, try to decide what I am going to do about our marriage.

I have always trusted Tad. In his job he has always had many meetings during the week. Now he has added a township board and other boards that require travel all over Michigan and a few to places like Bermuda. He used to be proud to have me along at the meetings out of town saying, "You are beautiful and I enjoy having you with me." Maybe he can only see the outside beauty. My outside is in a transformation but my insides are still the same. He now goes to these meetings by himself. I have asked him to his face, "What is wrong with us?" He just stares past me into space. I have even asked the painful question, "Are you having an affair or do you have a girlfriend?" He always answers, "No."

I need to work on me now, I need to heal from these cancer treatments then I can make other decisions. I married for a lifetime, did Tad?

I am joyous every day that I am alive. I pray each day that the man that said he wanted to spend his life with me until the end will share his life with me while I am still alive. These days of emotional exhaustion have taken the deepest cut into my heart and soul.

Our home has become a house, a place to hang your hat. Our house is too big. Tad seems to have too many rooms to move into and hide. Dear God, stay by my side. I need you with me on this journey.

> Teach me your way O Lord, and I will walk in your truth; give me an undivided heart, that I may fear your name. I will praise you. O Lord my God, with all my heart; I will glorify your name forever. For great is your love towards me; you have delivered my soul from the depths of the grave.
>
> Psalm 86: 11–13

> The Lord is righteous in all his ways and loving toward all he has made.
>
> The Lord is near to all that call on him, to all that call on him in truth.
>
> He fulfills the desires of those who fear him; he hears their cry and saves them.
>
> The Lord watches over all who love him, but all the wicked he will destroy.
>
> My mouth will speak in praise of the Lord.
>
> Let every creature praise his holy name forever and ever.
>
> Psalm 145:17–21

Sunday, September 14, 2003
sunny, blue skies

Last night, I dreamed that I was riding a horse over deep, emerald green grass. It was a beautiful place that had mountains and valleys and bright blue skies with white, puffy clouds. It was breathtaking. I looked up onto a ridge above me; and there, looking down at me, was Khanada. She was watching over me, protecting me, and keeping all the other horses safe. She was a radiant, brilliant white color. Her coat of snow-white fur glistened in the sun. She was so alert and joyful. Khanada galloped along the high ridge toward me to come closer. She stopped, snorted, whinnied, and shook her head with her long, flowing mane as if to wave and rode off with the other horses over the ridge.

God, thank you for the gift of dreams.

Saturday, September 20, 2003

Today, I went to an all-day women's retreat at a church that Tad and I used to attend twelve years ago. We had gone to this same church for at least ten years. I had played golf with some of these women. Many had children the same age as mine, and some had been patients at the dental office where I had worked. This was a tight-knit community, where each life touched and entwined the others.

I was asked to talk about my battle with cancer in front of a large group of women that could number in the hundreds. These women would know me, and I would know them intimately. The last time I had spoken into a microphone was when I had read Scripture in front of many of these same women at this church. I almost fainted into the podium out of total panic.

After being ask to speak at the retreat, it has taken weeks and weeks of prayer to get to the point that I could even consider speaking to a group of women, much less women that I knew. With the grace of God offering me my words, somehow I got through it.

Standing at the podium, speaking into the microphone in front of two hundred women that I knew, my first words, clearly and slowly, were, "I am a breast cancer survivor." To say those words out loud, into a microphone, brought goose bumps to my skin. Within seconds, I heard and viewed in front of me a roar of clapping thunder with friends rising to their feet.

The words seemed somehow by the grace of God to flow effortlessly from my mouth. It was the story of my battle with cancer to date and how I have leaned on God so much more than I ever thought I would or could. God has picked me up and carried me when it was no longer possible to go forward anymore.

The tears flowed like rivers from the audience and in my eyes also.

The other speaker's journey with God had been so much more powerful than mine. One woman had lived in Africa and had seen every man in her village—including her father, husband, brothers, and sons—murdered in front of her. The entire village was plundered and burned. She walked hundreds of miles with her daughters until she found a place where thousands of other women and their daughters lived together in horrible conditions. There, she gave up her daughters to missionaries to save them from starvation. They were eventually adopted by American families. She remained in Africa and worked with the missionary people in her own country. She became a strong believer in God and Jesus Christ. In the years that followed, she was asked to come to the United States and minister to Americans. Along the years, she was reunited with her then grown daughters.

This woman thought that *my* faith must be so deep to be able to come through what I had. God, was I put in her presence to keep me humble? I believe that today we have all been empowered to move forward in our relationship with God. It still amazes me every day how God is so powerful in my life that he walks with me in the shadows and brings me into the light. He is constantly by my side, holding my hand and carrying me when I can no longer walk.

> You are my lamp, O Lord; the Lord turns my darkness into light. With your help I can advance against a troop with my God I can scale a wall. As for God, his ways are perfect; the word of the Lord is flawless. He is a shield for all that take refuge in him. For who is God besides the Lord? And who is the rock except our God? It is God who arms me with strength and makes my way perfect.
>
> 2 Samuel 22: 29–33

> You, O Lord, keep my lamp burning; my God turns my darkness into light.
>
> Psalm 18:28

> Your word is a lamp unto my feet and a light for my path.
>
> Psalm 119:105

> When Jesus spoke again to the people, he said, "I am the light of the world. Whoever follows me will never walk in darkness, but will have the light of life."
>
> John 8:12

> This is the message that we have heard from him and declared to you: God is light; in him there is no darkness at all.
>
> 1 John 1:5

Sunday, September 21, 2003
sunny, clear, a hint of autumn is in the air

It has been about ten months since I was diagnosed with cancer. Today I went to church services, where I feel that God has a direct line through our preacher to me. Each sermon seems to be written by the hand of God for my teaching. Jonathan's sermons are, many times, about the issues that I have been dealing with that week. Jonathan delivers the service with feeling and conviction. Through Jonathan's sermon today, I feel that God has instructed me. He has told me what should be the appropriate course to take regarding the latest issue that I had been wrestling with in the week. It is extremely odd that I feel God that talks to me through Jonathan because I have never had these feelings with other pastors over the years. Maybe once in a while, in the past, I would feel like a sermon was directed toward me, but not with this intensity. I know that God talks to me through people and signs on trucks, billboards, and dreams. If I wasn't watching for his answers to my questions, would I have missed all of this?

Today, Tad and I took a fifteen-mile bike ride, one of many that I have taken this summer. It amazes me that I can do this kind of exercise. I must admit that the steroids that I have to take may be one of the reasons that I have as much energy as I do. These steroids reduce inflammation in my joints so that my joints can function at a less painful degree. My chest, neck, armpit, and back are burned from radiation; and I am extremely tired; but I wanted to spend time alone with Tad, so I rode. In seven more days, I will have the *final*, large, two-day radiation boost. Then I will be able to cross the finish line, hands held high in the air, *triumphant* against this disease called cancer.

Monday, September 22, 2003

The radiation wound on my neck is open and almost unbearably sore. On some days I feel my life has become creams, ibuprofen, prayers, prayers and more prayers. I am in such pain. I can hear Tad doing the dishes and picking up in the kitchen after we had the meal that I had prepared after work. I must go to sleep now. In the morning, work will be waiting for me as well as radiation, nurses, and a doctor.

Dr. Compassion, who is my radiologist, and the nurses at radiation are all so kind to me, so patient and very compassionate. They laugh and cry with me. These people physically and mentally ease the pain of burns and the emotional scarring of having a husband that can detach himself from me when I need him the most. Better days that are less painful are ahead for me. I can see the finish line now. This is when Tad said he would have a big, jubilant party for me. I see no party streamers, no laughter from him, and no joy. I am a survivor, and today I will celebrate. Today, I will wear *no wig* at work. My hair is *very* short; a salt-and-pepper color; and extremely soft, like a baby's hair. It is my hair, all *mine*.

The End of the Struggles and the Beginning of a New Life

Friday, September 21, 2003

I am off to stay at the Grand Hotel on northern Michigan's Mackinaw Island with Tad and others that he works with. Everyone that is going will be taking a spouse or friend and Tad wants to go, so he asked me. Tad has always loved this hotel and wanted to stay there because it has such a romantic atmosphere and now he has asked *me* to go with him. Could this be a new beginning to our plan after cancer? There will be a couple there that I know and she also had cancer about the same time I did. I have seen her at several of my appointments in the last few months and she has shared how helpful her husband has been to her. This should be an interesting weekend.

The weather was cloudy and forty-five degrees until about Cadillac. In Cadillac, the heavens broke open; and it rained buckets of rain. It may not be a weekend of walking and bike riding or golfing like I had envisioned, but Tad and I will be together. So I would think that it will be a nice weekend to reunite. There are not four words between us for the entire five-hour trip; just a cold, dark cloud hanging over head.

We missed the correct boat to the island. In a deafening silence, we waited for the next scheduled ferry. The trip over wasn't too rough or choppy, even with the wind and rain. Our room at the Grand Hotel was small but very nice. It was romantic to be in a hotel with such a vibrant and rich historic past. The Grand Hotel's front porch is purportedly the longest front porch in the world, at an estimated 660 feet that overlooks a formal tea garden as well as the resort scale Esther Williams swimming pool. I have always dreamed of staying here, but it is extremely expensive. This is a special treat to stay and not have to pay. Otherwise, I am sure that we would never be here. Romance and history is one thing, but money is another beast to Tad.

We met the group of people at the elaborate five-course dinner. The conversation was good, but the dinner was splendid. There was a dress code in the formal dining room which had an abundance of enormous bouquets of fresh flowers. The entire staff of male waiters was from either the Bahamas or Jamaica. We all had dressed appropriately—women in dresses and the men in suit jackets. Tad looked very handsome, and I felt extraordinarily beautiful sporting my own short, soft hair. I didn't hear a compliment, but I knew that it was great to be alive and almost finished with my treatments. We retreated as a few couples together to the copula to have a night cap and listen to the wonderful piano player. Usually, a person would be able to see for miles out of the glassed sides and roof, but the rain was coming down in sheets. It was beautiful on the glass with the lighting of the candles and the soft piano music playing. After a night of silence between Tad and I, and too much conversation with others, we retreated to our room and fell off to sleep for the night. Was this our romantic trip off to the islands alone together? This was wonderful but not exactly what I had in mind when Tad had given to me a leather case for my passport with a promise of a trip together to an island.

In the morning, it was very cold, only forty-five degrees and very windy. Tad was going somewhere, and he wanted to be by himself, so I decided to go for a horse ride. It had been a dream of mine to ride a horse on the island ever since I had been a small girl. Now, after almost finishing cancer treatments, I felt that I needed to do this *now*. I may never have this opportunity to do this again. I was scared. It was a wild weather day, and that usually means that the horses are wild themselves. But I *had* to do this.

I was nervous as I entered the stable and not many people were around. The weather was too crappy. I said, "I would like to ride, with a guide please." They asked if I had ridden before, and I said yes and that I have horses. In the same breath, I said, "I am healing from treatment for cancer and I don't want the horse that no one can ride because it is crazy." I asked for an English saddle, and they thought that I was crazy. I am so much more secure in an English saddle. I can feel the horse and his responses much better. There is not all of the extra saddle leather under my legs between the horse and myself. An English saddle was not available, for liability reasons; the compromise was an Australian saddle and a large, fun, level-headed mount.

The mission now was to find a trail guide. None had come to work yet, but there was a college girl who was a stable hand that knew the trails quite well and would take me alone. Awesome! We mounted and rode through the streets with that great clippity clop noise. Our hair was blowing wildly, and the mist was falling all around us as we rode our horses and visited. The trees twisted in the wind; the grasses bent to the earth as we galloped, jumped, and spoke of our hearts' concerns. This woman had recently had some great difficulties in her life. She had finished college and was preparing to leave for this summer job when her mother, a dental hygienist, was diagnosed with an aggressive breast cancer. Her Mom, after twenty-five years of marriage, had recently been divorced and was just getting her life together. Even though her mother had wanted her to go to the island, my new friend's greatest concern was that she should be at home with her mother. I assured her that, if her mother had said, "Go. I will be okay," she had meant it. There should be no more guilt feelings. I suggested just calling her mother and talking to her. I was sure that her Mom would be thrilled to hear from her.

God, how unique it is that you had put us together on this windy, cold, rainy day on an island in Michigan. This could have been my daughter. I explained that I also had been diagnosed with an aggressive cancer. I was finishing treatment next week and was a dental hygienist. We rode and talked for hours about our fears, the happy years, and what life might hold for us in the future. I felt so at ease speaking with this woman, like she was my daughter and I was her mother. It seemed uncanny how our lives paralleled each others. Would someday I be the divorced cancer survivor after over twenty five years of marriage? Only God truly knows. I really think that when we arrived at the stable, we both had found something in each other that would give us the strength to continue on. A great peace filled my heart. God, you work in ways I can't even comprehend.

> The Lord gives strength to his people; the Lord blesses his people with peace.
>
> Psalm 29:11

The Lord is close to the brokenhearted and saves those that
are crushed in spirit.

Psalm 34:18

Later in the morning, I met up with Tad. My cup was overflowing from my morning experience with God; this beautiful, young woman; and the animals in the woods. I wanted to
share the overwhelming beauty of the morning with Tad, and
he had no interest. It would only be his loss.

How could I be so fortunate to be alive still on God's earth?
We went for a bike ride around the island in the cool late morning, never saying a word to each other, the clouds still hanging
overhead. He was not interested in conversation of any kind.
In the previous years of our marriage, if we were on the island,
with or without children, it would always entail lots of laughter, bike racing, stopping to see a majestic view that God had
created, and always stopping to steal a kiss from one another.
Today, not even two words. Just pedal, pedal, and more riding the bicycles—only looking straight ahead, no stopping, no
laughter; and for sure not a stolen kiss. Is this my new life?

At least the buffet could always be enjoyed. So off we
headed to a meal that was a visual and a gastronomic feast at
the Grand Hotel. The table was fifty feet long. That would be
long enough for me to drown any sorrows that I had. I could
eat some of everything, and then I might feel better. We took
another bike ride after lunch to wear off the calories and then
took a nap in separate beds.

After dinner, we walked with other couples to a magnificent ballroom, where people were dancing and enjoying themselves. What a great way to wear off the calories again. This
was a beautiful turn of the century ballroom complete with a
band and well dressed couples dancing and thoroughly enjoying each other's company. This would for sure be an enjoy-
ment to Tad. We had spent the first half of our lives dancing
together at every chance we would get. It was always a great

chance to hold each other and enjoy the music together. In the '70s, Tad was the John Travolta of the country club. We were the *Saturday Night Fever* couple, the couple that everyone wanted to watch dance because we seemed to enjoy each other so much and the music just brought us together more deeply.

Dancing? This would be fun and loosen him up. I took his hand in mine as I had done so many times before and asked him to dance as I led him to the dance floor. Tad looked at me with terror and sadness in his eyes, and abruptly said, "That part of my life is over!"

I stared at this man that had been the love of my life for so many years and realized that our lives together were in great trouble. In public, in front of his friends he had shunned my affectionate gestures. At that moment I came to the realization that possibly no Grand Hotel, dancing, bike riding, or minutes with each other could cross this abyss that had formed between us. A great sadness brought me to my chair to sit and stare into the unknown future. God, what do you have in store for me? What is this great thing that you have promised? At this moment, I am not feeling like any greatness will ever be in my life. It was early, but we went off to bed, because only dancing would keep you up this late, and we are not talking or dancing.

As I lay my head on my pillow in my bed, I hear God's voice say, "Have faith in *me* and *trust!*" I awoke Sunday morning renewed in my faith and thankful that I have had this weekend at the Grand Hotel. After a fantastic breakfast, Tad and I were off to the ferry dock to catch a boat back to reality.

Monday, September 29, 2003
cold, dark, rainy, forty six degrees

Today, I have taken the day off because I have radiation today and tomorrow. These are my last two *boost* days of radiation.

The word *boost* makes my skin scream out in pain because the dose of radiation will be increased. These will be the last two days. My neck is so sore with blisters, bleeding, and dead skin. It hurts constantly and often I cannot get the cream onto the areas that I need to cover. But the good thing is that God has reminded me often in dreams and Scripture that he can heal our bodies. *Patience, rest,* and *faith* are the words that I hear from him so often these days.

I got up and cleaned out the closet for a few hours, and was so tired that I lay down and took a nap. Tad has taken a vacation day today so he could do yard work before winter sets in.

The area on my neck that is so bad hasn't been radiated in four days. I can't wear anything on that shoulder without it causing more pain and tissue problems. It is like the worst sunburn that you can imagine, and yet you still have to spend more time in the sun. I praise God that I am alive to feel this pain that will heal me.

My hands and feet are numb. My hair is a quarter inch long and a salt-and-pepper color. My clothes don't fit because I have gained weight. The best thing is that my family is healthy and so are my pets. I am grateful for every day that I have on God's earth. It's a good time to make some goals for the next year.

It just hit me that in one year's time, Tad has only hugged or kissed me maybe twice of his own free will. There were three other times that I asked for a hug or kiss and he reluctantly offered and many times I heard," I can't do that."

This has maybe been the most difficult thing of the entire cancer journey. Tad has completely detached himself from me. He has said that I am no longer beautiful and that I no longer turn heads. Heads only turn now he says if someone wants to see the fat woman with no hair and a smile. He has no use for me anymore. For richer and for poorer, in sickness and in health? They are only words. Only words.

I thank God each day that he has provided me with the family and friends that have been a wonderful help each step of the way. In the Bible, I remember reading that God has provided each of us with the people that we need in our lives to honor and fulfill the plan that God has for our lives. Thank you, God, for these people and especially my children. They are truly gifts from you. Now, if I leave the writing tablet and the pen on the table, dear God, will you write down the plan for my life so I can get it correct the first time? I hear the words, "Pray about it, Thais. Pray."

Tuesday, September 30, 2003
cool, partly sunny with fluffy, dark clouds on a blue sky, forty five degrees

I definitely feel and smell autumn in the air. I made my famous white chocolate raspberry cheesecake for Dr. Compassion and the workers that have helped me through radiation treatments. It is finally the last day that I need any physical treatment for cancer. I am only six weeks short of the date that I was first diagnosed. I guess that I had no idea that it may have to take one year to finish all of the treatments. I have been taking one step after another after another.

The day is really here. I'm happy, tired, excited, sore, burnt, fat, hairless, and did I mention, *joyful?* I need to rest now. I do love Matt, Laurelin, and Tad. I want many more joyful years with them.

Thursday, October 2, 2003
thirty three degrees

The morning temperature is so cold, *brrr!* The water in the buckets in the pastures was frozen. The sky was a clear blue. It was windy, and animal clouds floated above my head. These are the clouds that carry the essences of all those animals that have passed from this earth. They become a cloud; and only a few days a year, the clouds are in the shapes of these animals. These clouds look like horses, dogs, turtles, pigs, birds, and dragons.

Pollix and Pumpkin walked with me to the barn. They pushed their noses through the mountain of leaves that have accumulated each day. They love to roll and play even though each is old and now extremely slow to move. I am also, these days, extremely slow.

It was a very beautiful day. Dr. Rubie came to float Laddie's teeth. We visited while she worked. I hadn't seen her since Khanada had died. She always brings me joy; we visited, and I gave her some jewelry that I had made for her. I began creating jewelry when friends were so kind to exchange therapy for jewelry. This was great therapy for fingers that were losing their feeling due to drugs. Each piece of jewelry had a cross placed on it as a blessing for each person and to have us think of who is really in control. I don't have much energy, but I have great amounts of joy, and I can share it! I am grateful for the health of my family, friends, myself, and my animals each day.

Saturday, October 4, 2003
cold, clear, sunny

This is a beautiful morning. Today Tad and I went together to the big ski sale in Grand Rapids at Bill and Paul's. It was like a date and I enjoyed the time with Tad. I found a new jacket that will be my Christmas present from Tad. He shopped and bought some new things for himself.

Tomorrow, I will have known Tad for almost thirty years. We met at a friend's mutual wedding and both fell in love instantly. He put eighty thousand miles on his car that year coming to see me at college. It was an hour-and-a-half drive one way to college. He often visited after work, would stay for a short while and returned back that evening. He had gladly made those trips because we had a burning desire to be with each other even if for a few hours.

I was completing my degree in dental hygiene at college and was registering for dental school in Oregon when he popped the question. When we married, we had known each other about one year. Plans changed after the wedding, and Tad went back to school; so I didn't. It has now been almost thirty years! For some people, thirty years is a lifetime. Almost thirty years! He still hasn't hugged or kissed me in months; and if I hug or kiss him, he draws away. This is a sad way to spend the rest of my life, however many years I have left—especially after I have just spent the last year trying to stay alive. For what, for *this?*

I may have had two or three kisses and hugs in a year from him, but this is not how our first twenty years were. I was always so eager to go along with the program that he made for our family. After all, I think that when you dance, one person has to follow and one leads. I have seen a change in this last year; our plans have turned into his plan and only his plan. I have been working my entire life to always have something better in the future with him—always in the *future,* never living in the glory of what we have today because in his eyes, it will never be enough. *Never.*

He won't see a counselor. He says he is fine and doesn't need it. Tad and I for many years have happily enjoyed celebrating this day together. This year Tad didn't want to celebrate the anniversary of when we met. He said, "Those are just days in the past of my life, not something that I would celebrate now."

I am about celebrating anything that has to do with being alive. Tad had said that when I took off my wig forever, we would have a party with friends. It would be a celebration of being alive, of taking off my wig and a new beginning of life together. That was months ago, and I have heard of no plans being made for a celebration of any kind. He plans golf weekends with the guys and more weekends at meetings without me, meetings that many people take their wives and husbands to. I am alone again in a life with a husband that is living his own life on his own time in his own world; but I *am* alive.

Friday, October 10, 2003
sunny, eighty degrees

It is an exceptionally beautiful day! Wow. It has been so nice to be off work these last two days. Yesterday, I took a nice ride on Laddie. It was about seventy five to eighty degrees, in October, in Michigan! We rode out in the woods and through the fields. It was completely quiet, and no one was around. The burns from the radiation treatments are healing; and each day, I am feeling stronger. I am actually starting to be able to wear a shirt that touches my burns without great pain. This summer, I have ridden more miles on my bicycle than ever in my life. I think that I am close to seven hundred or a thousand miles. No wonder I am tired! If it weren't for the steroids, I'm sure that I couldn't have done that. I would think that I would be skinny. Maybe in another life but not this one. Today, I went to a trainer at the gym to start a workout program. I need to get more energy and less stomach.

Sunday, October 11, 2003
warm, gentle breezes, blue skies seventy five degrees

I went to church and then golf with Laurelin and Tad at Chikaming on this beautiful day. Soon, the winds will be screaming at our doors and the snow will be flying. "This is the day the Lord has made; let us rejoice and be glad in it" (Psalm

118:24) I am so joyful to be alive on God's earth. All of this beauty he has made for my pleasure.

> When I consider your heavens, the work of your fingers, the moon and the stars, which you have set in place, what is man that you are mindful of him, the son of man that you care for him? You made him a little lower than the heavenly beings and crowned him with your glory and honor. You made him ruler over the works of your hands; you put everything under his feet: all flocks and herds, and the beast of the fields, the birds of the air, and the fish of the sea, all that swim the paths of the sea. O Lord, our Lord, how majestic is your name in all the earth!
>
> Psalm 8: 3–9

Sunday, October 19, 2003
warm, sunny

It is one of those precious days of autumn in Michigan. After church, Tad went golfing with the guys so I went for a very nice ride on Laddie. There was no wind. We only have an outdoor arena, so we have to take advantage of all great days.

I have been trying to make jewelry for the church bazaar. I will donate these to the church. The people at the church have been so wonderful with prayers for me during my illness. Prayers are something that you can never get enough of. Shari continues to bring me meals, and she takes the time to show real concern about what she can do to help me. My hands and feet are still numb in spite of everything that I am doing to help restore the nerve endings. Sometimes, when I think of cancer, all of the treatments, and all of the decisions that have been made in this last year, it seems surreal. I can't believe that it was *me* that had cancer. When do I become a survivor? Am I a survivor now because I have finished the treatments or in five years, if I am still alive?

This is a warm, sunny, great day and a blue sky. I have so much to be grateful for.

Tad, Pollix, and I went for a walk at the dunes in Saugatuck. We have had Pollix for at least ten years and our children have grown up with him. He is about fourteen-years old. He also is deaf. He has been deaf for maybe four years. Pollix has learned to watch me for hand signals. He also has learned when he is out at night in our yard and I flash the porch light on and off that it is time to come inside. He is a very smart dog, but, like me, his body is giving out. He also is getting very slow, and it is difficult for him to walk very far. But he so loves the dunes. Pumpkin is very old and wants to go also but can no longer get into the car for the ride. She is a kind and loving animal. Pumpkin wants so badly to please me and to always be with Pollix and me, but she has so much pain and cannot go on this walk.

I came home after the walk and prepared a great dinner for Matt and Tad. Matt comes home occasionally from college to check up on me and give out all the hugs that I need.

God, I cannot thank you enough for these welcoming arms of my children.

Monday, October 20, 2003
sunny, and extremely windy, eighty degrees

What a glorious day to be alive. The flying leaves are everywhere in the air and on the ground. I went to the gym today. I am slowly healing on the inside and the outside.

I viewed a beautiful sunset with colors of indigo, shooting reds, vibrant pinks, and deep purples. Now the leaves are falling from the trees, so there is a clear view of sunsets and of the storms that roll across the fields. The immensity of the storms this time of year is overwhelming—God's power and majesty all rolled into one great thunderstorm with violent winds and torrents of rain. This is my time when I can just sit on the porch and watch the skies change and feel the temperatures shift, feel the rain on my skin and the winds dance through my hair.

Wednesday, October 22, 2003
partly sunny, windy, fifty one degrees

Each day, I am amazed at the beauty that God has created for me. I think of all of the wonderful, caring people that God has fashioned and brought into my path. The leaves, wind, sun, and each grain of sand created for my pleasure. Today, at work, I went for a walk at lunchtime. I am surely not as tired as I once was, but I still need more rest. Tonight, I made many pieces of new jewelry for the church. The bazaar will be soon, and I want to have as many pieces ready for them as is possible.

God still hasn't written anything down on the paper about the direction of my life. My thoughts wander and I contemplate: now that I have gotten through the cancer treatments when do Tad and I reap the great rewards of a closer relationship? Can we make it through sickness and in health, *together?* Or is my life to take yet another twist? He has become so distant and wants only to go to athletic events by himself. He says that he is going into the press box and I can't be there. So Tad's suggestion is for me to stay home. We have usually gone to all of the sporting events together. We also have always gone together to all of the continuing education courses that he attends. Now he says that he'll go to this one or that one alone. He wants me to stay home.

I am exhausted from clinical treatment, three surgeries, six months of chemotherapy, the extra week in the hospital, radiation, moving my children to college, and working four days a week, but it would be nice to go to a football game with him, like it used to be. After all, he is only sitting in the press box because he can, not because he is doing a job there. I do believe that if I had a supporting husband through all of these treatments the toll would not have been so great on my body.

I almost think that he might have a friend, one that is a woman near his age to comfort him in this "difficult time" he is going through. However, when I ask about our relationship, he says that it is fine and there is no one else in his life. Why is my heart breaking and my mind screaming at me? Something is not right. It will get better. Time heals all wounds, right? I am praying that he is telling the truth, for I have always trusted him in the past.

Thursday, October 30, 2003
glorious day, sixty five degrees

It is very quiet in our home with both children gone. A whole week has gone by. Mostly, I eat, sleep, work, work out at the gym, clean the house, and cook dinners for Tad and I when he is home. No housemaid here. When I asked Tad months ago if I could get someone to help once a month with the house-work he said, "It costs too much." Family, friends, and patients have been nothing but awesome to me as I have been on this journey. I don't work today.

This day is housework day—housework as in the laundry, cleaning, preparing the meals, and buying the groceries; the usual things for a day off. A day off of what? The other job? I picked up the house and went for a wonderful ride in the arena on Laddie. I usually don't ride if there is no one around, I especially would not be jumping. After being so close to death, would it matter now if I was to fall off and die? The sensible part of me said, "At least no jumping." We rode in the arena and through the fields. Laddie is starting to feel alive again. He trot-ted and cantered through the fields, past the fleeing pheasants that we had scared up. He is a glorious animal to share life with.

As I rode and thought about all that we have been through together, I thought about a quote that I once read in Ireland: "The soul would have no rainbows if the eyes had no tears." Is that why I love the Irish so? Well, as of late, I have experienced many tears. Thank you, God, for the rainbows.

Today was my last day with Jamie for a massage. Each time I see Jamie, she fills me with such incredible hope for a future, *my* future. She is going to Florida to help her mother. I told her that I had a dream that she wouldn't be coming back home because she had found a wonderful man to spend her life with. She laughed and said not to worry. "Thais that will never happen!" I will miss her. She has been a large part of the healing process for me, inside and outside.

Saturday, November 1, 2003
cloudy, overcast, fifty three degrees

I went for a ride on Laddie with our neighbors, Sara and Beth. We rode the fields and the gravel roads. It smelled of wet leaves, and the winds brought a chill into our bones. There was the exciting feel of the constant rush of the cool winds on our skin. You can tell when autumn is coming in Michigan. The winds shift, and the clouds begin to have a heavy, dark look. The sun seems to no longer be a frequent flier in the sky, and the leaves start to change colors along with the aromas in the air of burning leaves and cold rain. I wonder if when you get to the autumn of life there are so many signs to let you know that you are coming near the end of your seasons.

Tonight, as I am lying down to sleep, the cold, autumn rains are beginning to fall. It is a good night to sleep hard to prepare for the winter. God's way and plan is perfect. I may not know his big plan, but I know that *he* does. That is all that I need to know.

Taaa Daaaaa!

Sunday, November 9, 2003
clear, sixteen degrees

It was extremely cold last night and there was a full lunar eclipse. It was beautiful and scary at the same time. The earth took on the oddest color of darkness. I can see why people long ago were so afraid of evil happening during or after the eclipse. Yesterday, I went to see my friend ride in a horse clinic. She had purchased for me a package of riding lessons. These are lessons that I can take on her horse in the indoor riding arena. She has a wonderful horse that is well-trained in dressage. This was a gift to me for finally finishing cancer treatment.

Have I ever mentioned how cold my head has been all the time with no hair? I had to wear little caps to bed at night to keep my head warm while the rest of my body was in a major hot flash. Today, I will put away the caps because now I actually have hair. It is so long—all one inch of it—and getting wonderfully unruly. Tad has never touched my hair. Many of my friends want to touch it because it looks and feels so unlike my hair before.

Tad and I appear to have everything: the house, children, good jobs, the country club, friends and horses. Together, we have worked three jobs at once at various intervals to have all of this. I would have been happy with less of all of these things. It occurs to me again that he will never be happy because it will never be enough.

Wednesday, November 19, 2003

Last week, I had gone to lunch with Sandy. Sandy has been a friend since our boys were small. Andy and Matt grew up together, playing in the creek, catching fish, making tree forts, and camping overnight in our yards. The matches were after the BB, air guns, bow and arrows, spears for fishing in the creek, and tree forts. Who knows what someday they will confess to that happened in those years? It always astounds me at how many boys actually grow up when you consider what they get into over the years. Between Sandy, her husband Daryl and me, we tried to let the two of them experience growing up as we had: free and easy, slow and steady, with loving but watchful eyes from the parents.

By now, I had grown some very curly, salt and pepper, fluffy hair that looked much like a cotton ball that had been pulled apart. I now had a salt and pepper afro, but I am a light-skinned, freckled, middle-aged woman who did not know which products to use to control it. It is not pretty; but it is my hair, mine all mine. I am so proud of it but realize that it is getting a bit too unruly.

I met Sandy for lunch, and she had such a strange look on her face when she saw me. She had not yet seen my stunning new hairdo. Sandy was totally in awe. We talked and shared what had been going on in our lives since last being together. I shared that I loved having hair but it was so curly and unruly. I did not know how to style it, if that was possible. My hair was only about one inch long at its longest and salt and pepper in color and definitely not auburn. Sandy suggested that I go to see Benito. She said that he was a wizard with hair styles and color. She suggested that I stop in to see Benito and get an appointment with him. Sandy and I hugged with full tummies and warm hearts. Off I went with the address of Benito in my hand.

I pulled up through the slush and mush of another Michigan winter day, happy to be alive, into Benito's parking lot. It was an old house with a strobe light in the front window. It got my attention! I was expecting, when the door opened, a hot-looking, tall Latino man in a white suit with two-inch platform shoes on.

I turned the handle of the door; and there, in the middle of the room, under the disco light, stood a very handsome Latino man. He looked up, his dark brown eyes penetrated me, and I almost forgot why I was there. He stared at me and said, "Hello." I quickly remembered why I was there. "Sandy sent me to see if you could help with my hair." He looked at my masterpiece, my head of hair; touched it with his fingers; and looked into my eyes. "You had cancer, didn't you?" "Yes. How did you know?" "It is my job, baby." He said, "What do you want done?" At this point, I am so glad to have hair that cutting it wasn't even on my brain as an option. "I was thinking maybe some tips in how to control this work of art." Benito said, "I think that you were a redhead and should have the newest cut and style from New York." Bingo! He grabbed the swatches of hair color and chose very quickly, without any hesitation, my natural color. When I was modeling years ago, I learned to let the artists do their magic on me and just be quiet. I made an appointment for very soon.

Thursday, November 20, 2003
sunny, warm, windy, fifty seven degrees

Today, I see a beautiful blue sky and big, white animal clouds. What an awesome November 20! The best part is that I am here to see it. It will be one year ago tomorrow on a gloomy, rainy, November day that I began this journey through cancer treatment—a journey that I would never have chosen that has brought me to be incredibly deeper in my faith with God. I now talk and pray with him daily.

Today, I couldn't resist a ride on Laddie. The day was perfect for a ride, something that may not happen to much more due to the winter weather that will be coming soon. What a great gentleman he is.

My eyesight had gotten progressively worse with each chemo treatment. It is much more difficult to see now without contacts or glasses and to write in my journal. The writing is, at best, without contacts or glasses, illegible. It is now time to make a new eye doctors' appointment and see if he can improve my sight with a new prescription.

Today, for the gentle wind and the warm sunshine, thank you, God. This month, we have had over eight inches of rain. It is certainly time for a day of sun.

Friday, November 21, 2003
rainy, very dark, sixty three degrees

One year ago today, I didn't think that I would be alive to see this date. This is the date that I had gone for my mammogram to find out two hours later that I needed to return soon for an ultrasound and another mammogram. Today, the emotions came rushing back to me.

Now, at this date, my Mom is healthier. My Father is trying so hard every day to have a normal life after a massive stroke. I am *alive!* What a year! I have gone from healthy to having cancer. I have gone from having beautiful, long, auburn hair to being completely bald to having short, salt and pepper-colored, curly hair. I have sent two children off to college and gotten through difficult health issues with both. I have found out that my marriage is not based on a foundation in God or in love. I really don't know where God is leading me with all of this; and when I think about this year, I am again exhausted—emotionally and physically exhausted. I am a very strong woman, and I am alive. God told me to rest, and he will take care of the entire situation. My direct order is to rest. This I can do.

I awoke to a telephone ringing loudly next to the bed. When I answered it, I found that it was my friend. She was in a panic. She had just been diagnosed with breast cancer. God, now I know why I had to rest. We talked for hours, and she felt much calmer when we hung up. I must be strong for her.

Sunday, November 23, 2003

Travis's parents are alone without children on their once-a-year trip. This year, it is Mexico. My passport book that Tad gave me in the hospital just sits on my dresser, catching dust. That ten-dollar passport holder was given to me with a promise to go together soon to an island trip alone, just the two of us. That was almost a year ago, and I have heard nothing about a trip. I guess that it was a cheap, quick fix at the time for him.

On weekends, after working for four days, I spend my time cleaning, writing, and preparing meals. Of course, I am always trying to catch up on sleep. This healing thing takes much longer than I had ever dreamed. Since Tad seems no longer to want to share life with me, I guess this is a good time to rest and heal for whatever life hands me next.

Monday, November 24, 2003
snow, high of twenty seven degrees, wind chill of negative seven degrees

So much snow and it is the first of the season to stick. It is a cold and windy mess. It is the beginning of what could be a long winter. I am off to work early today sporting my new hairdo.

Last week was the day for my appointment with Benito. I was there on time. That was when Benito introduced me to the other hairstylist and assistants. The music was rocking, and we were the only people in the salon. Benito was calling out orders to the assistants to prepare this and that for my day with him. Benito can be very high-energy, and I had none.

I settled back for a day with Benito, putting all of my trust in him. He clipped, sprayed, and slopped goop on my hair. He talked about how cancer had touched his life, and I talked about how it had touched mine. I closed my eyes and let him massage my head while he washed my hair. The human touch is such a powerful thing. This man with the big, warm, piercing brown eyes was just what the doctor ordered. In a matter of hours, I had come to know a new friend that God had walked into my life. Benito insisted that he apply my makeup for the finishing touch. I felt like I was an eighteen-year-old model again. I felt beautiful again. Someone else was attending to my complete makeover. Benito gave me a mirror and smiled. Taaa daaaaa! It was amazing. I had been transformed into a beautiful woman with auburn hair. Granted, it was short hair; but wow did I look *hot* or what? I felt and looked like one million dollars, like a movie star. It was amazing. My day truly was a gift from Benito to me. I stood and turned to hug him; and he said, "Go show that husband that his girl is back!" I think that day; God was smiling down as he looked inside of a hair salon in Holland.

I drove home. My hair was covered with a scarf. I unveiled the "new" me to Tad, and he said, "That looks more like you." This was a good statement, but can the outside appearance be so important? Does he not realize that I am the same woman that left hours ago? I don't know, but maybe with this, I will see a change in Tad.

Tad smiled—no hug, no kiss, and walked into the other room to watch television. Or maybe this is not a new beginning. I walked into the kitchen alone to prepare dinner, looking like a model with no one to impress and no runway to walk on. I cried.

Now here I am, days later, sporting a new hairdo and at work on a Monday to see all of my great patients. At about midmorning, a husband of a friend came in for an appointment; and he told me that last week, his wife had been diagnosed with breast cancer.

Oh no. Here we go again. My heart aches for the family. She is younger than I am and has two small children. I must be strong for her. I will call her tonight and see if she wants to talk. *Cancer.* Why can't they cure it? *Cancer.* I hate that word. I will pray for strength and healing for this family, pray that God armors them with what they need for a long battle. We must both have the strength of being in the Lord's hands.

> God is our refuge and strength, an ever present help in trouble. Therefore we will not fear, though the earth give way and the mountains fall into the heart of the sea, though its waters roar and foam and the mountains quake with their surging.
>
> Psalm 46:1–3

> The Lord is my strength and shield; my heart trusts in him, and I am helped. My heart leaps for joy and I will give thanks to him in song.
>
> Psalm 28:7

For who is God besides the Lord? And who is the rock except our God? It is God who arms me with strength and makes my way perfect. He makes my feet like the feet of the deer; he enables me to stand on the heights. He trains my hands for battle; my arms can bend a bow of bronze. You give me your shield of victory; you stoop down to make me great. You broaden the path beneath me, so that my ankles do not turn.

2 Samuel 22: 32–37

God, Is This Why You Have Prepared My Faith?

Tuesday, November 25, 2003
sunny, blue skies today, white puffy clouds, sixty degrees

It is late at night and has been almost a year since I was diagnosed with cancer. I am reflecting on this last year of my life. Thinking of how cancer has impacted my life and all of those around me. Cancer is not something that I would have chosen to clarify my life, but it has. I have begun to understand the meaning of *my* life much more clearly. It is becoming more obvious who should be in my life and who should not. Who is still there for me when the going gets incredibly tough and who is not. I am facing a possible divorce when I am not strong enough to do so and Tad obviously is.

After having cancer treatments, when do you actually become a survivor? Would it be after treatments are finished or after you try to reestablish a life out of the chaos that cancer has left? My father is fighting for his life and trying to fight for mine. I can see each day that he is losing ground with his struggles to keep a failing body alive. His mind is sharp and he never complains about test after test and the inability to move on his own. Dad and I have had deep discussions about living and dying. He is at peace with the inevitable truth that each of us should face before we are confronted with it, the truth that every person has in common; *we will all die someday*. We live in a circle of life, some of our circles are large and others very small but each has a beginning and each will have an end.

Have we prepared and lived our lives knowing that this is a truth? Or have we just existed each day as if we will always have another? Have we been as kind to others as we could have? Have we found and used the talents that we were given to reach our greatest potential whatever it maybe? Or have we sat back and blamed everyone and everything around us for not achieving what we thought should rightfully be ours? Have we rushed ahead stepping on anyone who gets into our way to accomplish what we thought we should achieve for ourselves? As humans we have feelings of invincibility and immortality but our existence is far more tenuous than we may think. Have we built up our defense barriers so greatly around our innermost feelings that no one, even those that love us the most could break down the walls around our hearts?

I have learned that it is not always the achievements of great scale and proportion that define our beings as much as the tiny ordinary things and people in our lives, when put together makes our lives so immensely worth living. That is when the ordinary becomes the extraordinary and heartfelt joy is contagious to others.

I have no idea how long I will live or what I will face here in this world before I die. I do have the realization that God does know these things and if I am looking for a guide in my life, a lighthouse in a storm, God will be that for me. When I need a focus, a mentor to complete my life, God will be mine.

I have also come to the understanding that we may never *know* why things happen in our lives in a way that we hadn't planned. I do appreciate that we as humans do have the choice of free will. The will to make the best out of a difficult situation and respond as if the world is a training ground for something larger. Something more wonderful than I can even imagine. If my cup were half empty I would always be taking from it and end up with nothing. Possibly with a cup one half full I could be trying to fill it at the expense of others? Yes, my cup is large and always half full. For then I have the possibilities of filling it with more joy each day because I am content with a one half *full* cup.

I thought that my life was full and complete, but God has taught me to revaluate what is important and what gives life itself to the meaning of *being alive*. I have begun to volunteer in ways that will help others who may be going through what I have. I have no idea what trials lie ahead but God please tell me if I am on the right path?

Last night I fell to sleep thinking of my Dad, praying, and asking God what I was to do about a life that may have so many uncertainties to work through when I should be healing from this last year.

As I slept, my father came to me in a dream. I stood on a muddy road full of potholes and ruts that were so deep that they could swallow a car. The road was very winding and twisting, narrow at points and extremely wide at others. To the sides of the road were bodies of water, some calm and serene, others turbulent. Between the bodies of water were trees and forests. Some trees had large, long-reaching branches that appeared to look much like very gnarly, uninviting arms. These arms gave the impression that they could reach out and capture me if I strayed too close to the edge of the road. Within the forests and bodies of water, there was quicksand and great amounts of it in various places.

All of this was very confusing and frightening. As I stood there, surveying these sights alone, it came to me that I must be in the wrong place. I looked up far off into the distance at what appeared to be the end of the road, and standing there was my father. He appeared to have an aura of brilliant, white light around him. I found this sight comforting in the midst of my rising anguish. Dad held out his hand to me. I looked at him and said, "Is this the road that I am to follow, the path I am to take? Is this the road that leads to the rest of my life?" Dad smiled and looked straight into my eyes and said, "Yes. This is the road that you are to follow." I returned with, "*Why?* Why do I have to follow a road with so many frightening things? Any one of these things could end my life at any time. I am scared and cannot do this alone." Daddy looked at me with his hands and arms stretching out to me with a magnificent light showing all about him. He said, "Yes, this is the road, and you will *not* be alone. *We* will be with you every step of the way."

I stared at Daddy as I tried to put my mind around the fact that this horrible path in front of me was the one that I was to walk. I whispered to Dad, "*We?*" He said, "Yes, Thais, *We*. You need only to take the first step." At that moment, from the end of the road, Daddy's hand reached out for mine; but from above me a warm, very large, safe hand came to rest on my shoulder as yet another came from heaven to hold my outstretched hand. I was holding the hand of God, and he was holding mine. God and my Father were willing to stay by my side no matter what I was to be going through in the future. I knew that the road of re-establishing a life after cancer could not be easy. This was not the road I had chosen. I knew that with God guiding the way, it was possible. This was one moment with God and then I took a deep breath.

This is my prayer God: "That you hold onto me so tight that I may *always* be with you no matter how much I may stumble and no matter what happens in my life. Please walk so close to me that I may feel your breath on my skin."

Looking toward my father and holding on tightly to the hand of God, I took that first giant leap of faith into the rest of my life.

Epilogue

My story here would not be complete without the understanding of what has transpired in my life since this journal was written.

Yes, I did go on to have a divorce after thirty-one years of marriage. As a matter of fact, my daughter was engaged about eight weeks before my husband filed for our divorce. Her wedding was August 5. Our divorce was final four weeks later. I went on to help move my daughter and her husband to Boston; and within two months, I also helped Matthew move to Boston. Tad was busy on both dates.

Our home sold shortly after Laurelin's wedding; and I, with friends and family, moved into the most beautiful gift of a home that God could provide for me. About a year later when I was beginning to establish my new life, I had a freak accident.

I had a double skull fracture, multiple facial fractures, a fractured elbow, a torn retina, and a traumatic brain injury. I had bled unconscious for nine and a half hours. As the doctor put it, "You are lucky to be alive and must have had a host of angels watching over you." My reply was, "Both of my father's in heaven were working overtime on me that night."

It took months of therapy for me to seek out the word I was looking for and to speak entire sentences. When able to return to work, I lost my position.

I have compiled this book with years of physical therapy and hundreds of visits with doctors. God is truly the author, and I am the co-author. God continues to walk with me daily and at times has carried me through continuous legal matters, taking care of my home, and restoring my health. He has shown me many gifts that I have only come to know through these trials.

My life has gone on to establish new relationships; increase my health; and with each day, increase my faith and understanding of God. I continue to journal daily. I have been blessed with the gift of family and friends. Through them, I have been offered the opportunity to experience life as God's plan has intended, leading me to step through the rest of my life with God one moment at a time.

I now volunteer with groups such as The American Cancer Society, Love Inc., The City Mission, Women in Transition.